The Change You Want

Is

Within You

Sister Magdalene Musau

The Change You Want is Within You

Year of Publication 2021

ISBN: 978-9914-700-46-6

The Change You Want

Is

Within You.

Sister Magdalene M.
Musau (RSM)

To my great biological family

and the entire mercy family.

All you who have crossed my path of life,

my great teachers who have contributed to 'my waking up!'

For all who gave me the lessons that have helped me expand

my reality and options.

My unwavering friends

and relations who always have my back!

Table of Contents

Table of Contents

FORWARD

To say "we want change" is easy. To actually CHANGE FROM WITHIN - to break the cycle and patterns of our parents, family, ancestors and culture - is something else entirely.

It takes a person of courage and conviction, like Magdalene Musau. I have had the good fortune to meet and to work with Ms. Musau in a program that I lead. She has the kind of presence and magnetism that attracts one's attention as soon as she walks into the room. She is charismatic, funny, poised, and deep. She is a born leader who has integrated the lessons of her life into a powerful vision and mission to help others get out of their destructive patterns, patterns of behavior and attitude that keep them from growing into the people they were really meant to be.

When she asked me to write the foreword to her book, 'The Change You Want is Within' I didn't hesitate. It is an honor. In this book, Ms. Musau has courageously laid herself bare. She uses the experiences of her life to open up conversation and reflection, and invites readers to ask questions about their own life in order to consider new perspectives and pathways to change.

This is a generous, thoughtful and deeply personal book. And one that doesn't shy away from the difficult topics that many of us live but don't want to talk about: domestic violence, HIV, abandonment, alcoholism, genital cutting, death and caretaking our parents. What more exemplifies self-awareness and true personal growth than turning a life full of fear, despair, poverty, and strife into a reflection on how to not just survive, but how to thrive?

In the process of reflecting on the challenges of her childhood, Ms. Musau honors Mellie, a woman who suffered abuse and poverty, but nevertheless made sure her children got an education and had opportunities she herself did not have. She also honors the cultures and traditions that shaped and enriched her, seeing herself as part of a complex and beautiful tapestry that embraces the very best of her ancestors and culture.

Thank you Magdalene, your book will do that thing that good books do-make a difference in the lives of your readers. Thank you for making the choice to use your experience as a gift to others. It is a brave choice, a loving choice and a wise choice.

Ann Bradney

Director,

Radical Aliveness Institute

Los Angeles, California

~ CHAPTER ONE~
EXPERIENCE: 2015

Have you stopped lately and wondered who you are at present?
Do you need to appreciate anything at all in your life right now?

The sun beautifully colored the horizon orange and the dew shone like light reflecting off fields of shattered glass. The many birds in the trees were chirping melodiously as the sun's rays warmed and soothed her body. The mooing of cows and bleating of goats could be heard across the fields. By this time, eleven all animals were out of their sheds.

Mellie was basking in the young morning sun. Its early morning rays warmed her back as she sat under the jacaranda tree, one of the many on her compound. It was coming to the end of the dry season and the trees were budding, slowly raining down their small purple flowers, shaped like tubes to entice the insects. Their aroma filling the air indicated the coming rain.

The people here were farmers and the rain meant life for the earth that had been thirsty for over three months. Mellie knew from experience how to read the changing behavior of the trees to interpret the weather. In her youth, she would have been preparing the fields by now and she would be working the day's long hours. But she was no longer in her youth and she had earned herself some long-deserved peace and rest.

The wind moved a few of the falling petals onto Mellie's head. She got distracted as she got a glimpse of a bee collecting pollen from the newly fallen flower. Momentarily she caught sight of many others buzzing away as they superbly concentrated on each flower, their legs laden with their fine harvest.

She was sitting just outside her six-roomed, brightly painted house. Inside it was too cold. Traditionally the house would be roofed with thatched grass but nowadays it was seen as a sign of development to have an iron roof and so that was what she had. The grass would keep the house cool during the day and trap the warmth at night. The iron did not and so it was too cold in the house that particular morning.

Her house faced eastwards, towards the main river which flowed approximately a kilometer away. The next home was far from hers and only intermitted dotted iron roofs among the trees hinted at the existence of neighbors. The land was terraced towards this river, which cooled the wind as it travelled up the hill towards Mellie. She shivered a comfortable shiver as she felt the wind flow around her. To the north stood one lone hill from which this village got its name. It was called Kilima Pekee in Kiswahili meaning *Lone Hill*.

She would sit there until the sun lulled her into a doze in the sunshine. She had nothing to do this morning and nowhere to be, nobody to see. She reached for a small pocket mirror. As she looked in it, she could see how she had changed and more especially internally. She saw all the wrinkles on her face. Her irises had white rings around them. 'This was new,' she thought, wondering what it meant. Her heart felt different though.

The Change You Want is Within You

Mellie remembered like it was yesterday her smooth, rosy cheeks and mouth full of her natural teeth. She laughed as she lowered the small pocket mirror. She tilted her head as she shifted the mirror to catch a better view of her whole face. She turned till she could see a better reflection of her face. Thoughts of her youth filled her with electrical excitement and nervousness. Her laugh broke the still of morning and she looked around – as if shocked by her own elation – to see if anyone had heard her.

Her wrinkles were not the only thing different about her now. She no longer wore her arm-length bangles and her long earrings. These used to be part of her routine dress. The multi-colored bands of her bangles, yellow, silver, red, blue, green, used to hit against each other as she worked, creating a nice resonation. Her earrings, equally colored, used to dance with the wind and the movement of her head. She sighed and wondered to herself who this woman was that she saw in the mirror.

Thoughts of zest and zeal crisscrossed her mind like swords in a battlefield. She was too busy engrossed in her world of thoughts to notice her daughter-in-law, Margarita, who emerged from the smoky kitchen that sat opposite the main house. The kitchen was grass thatched. Margarita rubbed her stinging, teary eyes as she exited the smoke and approached Mellie. Margarita was a good daughter-in-law. She was hardworking caring, generous and hospitable too. Margarita had lived with Mellie since her early years of marriage. As a consequence, they had developed some convenient relationship.

"Mama," Margarita asked her through her stinging eyes, "what makes you laugh till your molars show?"

Mellie dismissed the question with a wave of her hand. “Ah! It is nothing of importance.”

Her daughter-in-law picked up a few sticks for the fire and disappeared into the smoking kitchen again. Soon after, Mellie fell back into her bangle of thoughts, shifting and flicking from one memory to another.

She was not fond of memories, Mellie. They made her shake like a blade of grass up against a whirlwind. Her story began to unfold in her mind like a gently peeled onion; one layer after another, slowly, carefully.

Reflection time

What needs to be healed in your life?

When you look back on your life, where have you come from?

How could you ensure the elderly in your life are taken care of?

~CHAPTER TWO~
MELLIE'S FAMILY

Have you felt valued in your family as a woman or a man?
What are you grateful for as you think of your origin?

It is said 'Educate a woman and you educate a nation'. I add, semi educate an intelligent woman and let us take a long journey into the memory line of a semi-educated woman and see.
According to the Collectivist Culture in Kenya, and more so, in the Kamba culture characterized by male domination at many levels in the past, when a husband died, the wife was inherited by the husband's brother, changing her name and becoming his wife. When Mellie's father died, her mother was inherited by Mellie's uncle and thus became married to him. This was the norm and hence there was no cause for alarm. It was a custom followed to the letter to ensure the continuity of a man's name even after his death. The children born to his brother by that wife would be called after the deceased man.

It was also done to ensure widows and their children, if they had any, were taken care of. Therefore, Mellie's father, her new father, ended up with four wives by the end of his life – three inherited and one by his own accord. Mellie belonged to the last wife and all her cousins became her stepbrothers and stepsisters. There was no distinction between cousins as they now had become siblings. They all belonged to the same father. In the Kamba language, the word for cousins is *mwanaasa* or *mwiituaia* [son or daughter of my father or mother]. So, there were no cousins, only siblings.

Mellie's mother had only three daughters with no son. In the course of childhood, boys went through circumcision to initiate them into adulthood. During childhood also, all girls underwent female genital initiation for the same reason. The boys' initiation was assumed normal and expected. For the girls it was believed a necessity, to keep them 'faithful' to their husbands. Initiation was something one was supposed to yearn for and be proud of. It brought the initiate a sense of being and belonging. The blood that was poured from the initiation was seen as a libation and it even went beyond the living in a spiritual way to connect the initiates to the ancestors and then to God. One had to undergo it for self-identity but more importantly for one's community. If one endured the pain with courage, they were respected and honored as heroes and heroines.

All three girls underwent this ritual as it was normal practice at the time. Mellie was the youngest of the three girls. Kam, the middle child, died as a teenager but the oldest daughter, Malia and Mellie were both educated by the missionaries. Christianity was spreading throughout the land, especially from the mission in Kangundo. With this Christianity came some education and Mellie had access to this education. Mellie's mother, a convert to Catholicism and a believer in the Mzungu (white) education made sure she went to school. It was she who took Mellie to the mission school. The other girls besides her own in her family and extended family did not have this conviction.

The bribe of a handful of sugar given to each student for attending class each day was an added advantage.

A petal fell on Mellie's nose and woke her from her memory dream. She smiled as she shifted slightly to ensure she remained under the shade of the jacaranda tree. Her memories were flooding back to her now. She remembered joking with her classmates as she sat in school. They were learning phonetics in Kiswahili and accents of some students meant they struggled significantly. The rest of the students would laugh as the Mzungu priest teaching the class would ask them to say "fa". They all would, except one student who would respond "mba". He was older than the rest of the students, not having started his education until his early twenties. At that age, it was difficult for anyone to recognize the differences between subtle words and sounds. Again, the teacher would repeat "sema (say) FA" and again the student would lift his head up, distorting his face as he tried, as he stressed hard only to shout.

"Mba".

Now Mellie knew the difficulties of his late education. Had she known then what she knew now she wouldn't have laughed. But children can be unintentionally cruel. She laughed because, as a child, she found it funny. It was strange the memories which stay and memories which leave.

Reflection Time: Culture

What is your experience of wife inheritance?

Was the practice of genital cutting positive or negative?

~CHAPTER THREE~
THEIR CONTEXT

The beliefs you hold now were made at a certain time in your history.
The situation was different from today so you may need to change your beliefs to suit the reality you are in now regarding the losses in your life.

How do you cope with grief in your life?

Having attended the mission school, Mellie could speak Kikamba and Kiswahili fluently and could write it well too. She also had some English vocabulary. She was equipped for life, unlike the majority of her age-mates. The man she was to marry, too, was educated. And more than she. He could communicate in his mother tongue Kikamba, Kiswahili and English.

Fredrick, Mellie's suitor and eventual husband, was expected to pay a certain number of heads of cattle to her parents or, in their demise (as was true in Mellie's case) to the first-born son. It had to be the eldest of the living siblings. Since Fredrick had a little more education than most people at that time, he had gotten a prestigious job with the East African Railways Company and was more than capable of this payment.

In the years before the 1950's the East African Railway Company was the place to work. The other option was to join the colonial government army. Fredrick had a salary and lived in the capital city Nairobi and was better off than most people.

And so, Fredrick was able to fulfil the marriage requirements with ease. He and Mellie wedded in the Catholic Church. The church was built by the Holy Ghost Missionaries from Ireland. It sat in a green valley surrounded by three hills. There were two rivers on either side of the church compound providing the area with plenty of water. From the entrance, one was welcomed by a beautiful parish farm with all kinds of tropical trees laden to the ground with abundant fruit and crops. To the furthest end were stalls for cows and goats and a chicken house. For the men of the cloak, this place was a haven to come to at the end of the many hours of travel through paths and tracks to bring the Gospel to the vast parish.

When Christians came here it felt like home. The air around the church was cool most of the day compared to the rest of the hot region. There were many trees, shrubs and beautiful flowers. This would provide a nice background for their wedding photos. They both loved photos. She remembered those beautiful flowers she held on that wedding day! At this memory, she rolled her eyes and slightly tilted her neck and she flirted as on her wedding day. It left her with a shy smile.

At the rear end of this church was a huge iron bell. It was elevated some meters above the ground. It weighed at least a hundred kilograms. A mass server had to pull a strong nylon rope which hung an arm's length from the floor. Sometimes two boys had to swing on it to make the bell sound. One could see their legs hanging in the air as they attempted to exert their weights towards the ground so that it could gong. It could be heard from the ridges and valleys over twenty kilometers away. It tolled at six in the morning, at noon and six in the evening. Catholics were supposed to stop and recite the angelus when the bell tolled.

The church itself was simple redbrick with an iron roof. A pre-Vatican Council white marble altar was built from the front wall. The priest offered mass with his back to the congregation. There was no electricity so a kerosene lamp sat beside the tabernacle as an indication of the Blessed Sacrament. On the walls of the church were pictures depicting the Way of the Cross, typical of many catholic churches. Most of the images were of white people though showing Christianity still as a foreign religion at the time.

Mass was offered in Latin as was much of Mellie and Fredrick's wedding. About two hundred people could sit in the church, on wooden planks with no backrests. Marrying in a church proved their commitment and seriousness to the Roman Catholic faith. Good and practicing Catholics were encouraged to marry in the church and so they did. If anyone did not, the bell would not toll for them when they died (normally, the church bell tolled when a catholic died). Such a person would be "considered dead" as far as the church was concerned.

The new Christian faith preached against most African practices and in this context the Kamba practices. They were termed as 'pagan'. Actually, this area was the location of the 'head shrine' for the traditionalists. Shrines were also made in good natural forest areas with beautiful sceneries. God was believed to like nature which had not been meddled with. The missionaries had come to build a parish in this area to convert these people ingrained in this culture. As a matter of fact, drums were heard from six in the evening till six the next morning as 'Kilumi' (a Kamba Religious Ritual) dancers played the drums and danced to appease the deities. As Catholics themselves, Fredrick and Mellie didn't want to be mistaken as 'pagans' or their sympathizers. They had to show their stance as having forsaken all these former ways of their fathers! After all who wanted to be treated as a pagan? Definitely not Fredrick or Mellie.

In the 1940s, when Fredrick and Mellie wedded, a movement was occurring. The land where Mellie and Fredrick grew up was becoming too crowded. According to the tradition, men-owned vast areas of land and children were born to provide labor to work the land. The more children one had, the richer they were considered. Mellie's clan were farmers who once lived in Kangundo, one of the most fertile areas in Kamba land, Kenya. This area had a favorable climate and good soil and so produced good yields of crops each year. As a result of the fertility of the land, the population increased immensely. The land was subdivided to account for the increased population and the area of land owned by each individual shrunk.

Because of this, the colonial government began a movement to decongest the overly populated Kangundo Area and relocate the villagers to another settlement scheme in the now Makueni County of Kenya.

It was for this reason that many people, including the recently married Mellie and her husband, migrated away from their home to the less populated areas of Kamba land.

Makueni was a jungle of a place. Originally a national park home to all kinds of animals large and small. It got its name from the enormous poisonous snakes – known locally as the Makuua – that lived there. These were not one single species of snake, but were many: Pythons, Puff Adders, Black Mambas, Saw Scaled Vipers, Black-Necked Spitting Cobras and more. An 'ikuua' (a single one) was any of these deadly snakes which resided in the jungles of Makueni.

Herds of elephants, giraffes, zebras, antelopes and prides of lions and all manner of other creatures lived there too. For those forced to relocate, it was a difficult move and many died trying, usually from snake bites or scorpion stings. So, people knew herbal medicines as a remedy for the various health challenges they faced including poison. The nearest hospital was many miles away.

Since Fredrick had a salary, he was able to travel there to acquire as much land as he could clear among his kinsmen who served in the local government. But they did not move to the land at that time. Instead, they lived for some time in Nairobi City. Because of Fredrick's job, they had the freedom to move when and where they wanted.

Underneath the jacaranda tree, Mellie winced slightly as her memories took her further into nostalgic space. In Nairobi, she had her first pregnancy. It was a miscarriage. Mellie didn't like talking about death. She found this unforgettable. When asked she would hold up her hands and shake her head from side to side, blinking back tears. 'Just let that lie', she would say inaudibly. She believed that stories about grief were better laid to rest. Later on, in her life, a life marred with violence and suffering, she would continue to stand by these words.

She picked up a sweater she had been knitting lately to keep her loneliness and thoughts at bay. 'This can nearly fit my grandson', she thought. 'Just a few more lines of knitting'. She loved to care for people and particularly loved her grandchildren. It was the pride of parents to see the continuity of life, the continuity of their name. Her grandson, Fredrick, was named after her deceased husband and she loved him dearly. Mellie was not able to bring herself to face the painful side of her life. Some things, she thought, were better forgotten. Grief and pain for her were no-go-zones. It was the way she protected herself. The way she ensured she remained sane. It is said the brain has a survival technique of blocking intense pain. During the young couple's life in town, they dined and kept company with the rich. The wives had a circle of friends who did things together like buying their clothes from the same boutique – it was the only boutique in their local town.

They would bake, knit and visit each other's homes for celebrations. Her husband cared for her greatly and made sure she had all she needed. The husbands met for a drink as they shared stories about their culture but mostly about the colonial situation in the country. But after a few years in town, she tired of the city and yearned for the countryside. It was where she was born, where she was raised and she decided it was time to go, develop and take care of her home in Makueni. Their destination was always to be Makueni. The town was only temporary.

In the village was a certain woman, believed to be a witch. She was a short, stout woman who spent her days preparing an alcoholic brew and ensuring her clients stayed hooked in her den. She made sure the brew was ready at all times of day or night. At times Mellie could not help thinking this woman had become jealous of Fredrick and cast a spell on him. It was the only way she was able to make sense of his change of behavior. Why else would he take up the drink, why else would he submit himself to such shame, with many – including his neighbors – knowing where he was and what he was doing? This witch was a mean, selfish and jealous woman. She wanted nothing more than the destruction of others for her own gain. Whether or not she was a 'real' witch was irrelevant. Fredrick was under some sort of spell. And everything else held constant, she was the likeliest cause!

Fredrick was a tall and handsome man. He had a nice slender body. Generally, he said little and did not talk about his past. But when he drank he spoke uncontrollably and over time, before anyone could realize or understand why he began to drink like a fish, coming home late at night, stumbling around and yelling. When he was silent it was screaming silence. When he was drunk, Mellie found out why. She found out about the secrets of his family.

Over time Mellie learned that Fredrick had a cupboard of skeletons. It was possibly too scary even for him to begin to look at. His own father had been murdered in a family feud over his mother. He was the firstborn and his young sister was a toddler when their father died. Apparently, his father's cousin was interested in his mother. So, it was said that when they went looking for pasture far away from home – this took them several months until the rains came – the cousin got the opportunity to attack and kill him. Mellie did not find this out until a certain kinsman shared the information. He said Fredrick's father was killed in a "sinful situation", a silencing statement that ended any further enquiry on the matter.

Fredrick's father had no brothers and so, as was the tradition, his mother married the next closest relative, his cousin, the man who everyone knew had murdered Fredrick's father. Though the family moved in with the cousin, they still kept their father's name, a constant reminder of what had happened. It was a shameful reality for Fredrick to admit. The ill-feelings were however carried through the generations but only as a big family secret. Only when he was drunk would he stumble around shouting, "I'm the legal son of" without ever finishing the sentence.

This was just before Mellie moved to Makueni. As Fredrick was to stay behind for work and come later, these random moments of drunkenness and past revelations ended when Mellie moved and life continued on as normal, more or less. Mellie was a farmer and the new land was virgin and hence quite fertile. She minded the farm and, as Mellie was very industrious, the land responded generously to her hard work. Within no time she had lots of cattle. She was mostly alone as her husband continued to work in the city, coming to Makueni and the home only occasionally. She carried a second pregnancy to term and the baby was delivered at home. Mothers often delivered at home with the help of a well-seasoned midwife. This child, Tinda (which means the one who took longer to arrive), had been choked by the umbilical cord during birth and by the time the midwife could cut it off, the little angel was dead. He may have taken longer to arrive, but he definitely did not take long to leave! Now Mellie had two children who had died before they could live.

Mellie was very distressed and did what she knew best. She pushed this immense pain into the depths of her unconscious.

Kamba, the tribe to which Fredrick and Mellie belonged, believe in death as a passage. Death was seen to be so near humans and yet when it happened it was pushed far away and sometimes people went into silence. Mourning was done through talking in low voices as people, especially women, sat together on the floor or ground. When there were deaths, discussion of them was buried with the dead. Mellie, like others, believed that God gave and also took back. It was God's will. The same God who took away would give again. Life had to continue. There was no point crying over spilt water. That was how she saw death. Talking about it was like opening the coffin that she preferred to leave alone. She said in desperation, "there is no point, there is no need. Leave it alone!" All she knew is that she had to hang in there... she had to stay afloat!

She tries and she bares
She cries and she bears
It's clear that she is more than this for she cares
For her two lost children dares

The pain she can and has kept
For this, she has often wept
It's been a long-term dream
For within she is the top of the cream

She knows all her duties
But not without difficulties
More than just chores in the kitchen
She'll stay afloat so listen

Reflection Time: Death and Grief

The body's natural way of dealing with too much pain is to fight, flee or freeze. What are the upsides and downsides to these methods?

Are there other ways to deal with the pain?

It is not unusual to see people who have had intense loss holding on for years on something that keeps them in connection with the deceased one. It is important to notice how we cope with death. Then we can see warnings of needing help to help us cope.

Have you ever attended a funeral of known or unknown people and realize you can't stop crying? This may be a sign you still need healing from your losses.

What are the deaths you need to face in your life?

What do you do when faced with death?

Do you need to talk about those deaths you fear facing?

Could you have developed a medical issue after the death of a close relative or partner? How could it be related to your grief?

Could you have transferred your attention to someone else or something else to avoid dealing with the loss?

~CHAPTER FOUR~

DOMESTIC VIOLENCE

Domestic violence can often be a shameful topic to engage with, in families. It exposes the members and they lose face. As a result, it often remains a family secret safely kept. Yet it continues to affect those keeping the secret.

This is for all;

Children who don't know who they are because the
Big people's words and deeds in their lives
Have adulterated their image
They have forgotten who they are.

Those who have gone to bed earlier than usual.
Or left home unwillingly because it is unbearable
Or even stayed back for the sake of peace
Someone knows how it feels like

The hearth is lifeless!
So, you may not eat tonight
Or the stove and the cutlery is strewn on the floor
From last night's parents' fighting episode

You do not know when to smile
You whose antennae always go up
Because you sense something is about to happen
Go to bed not sure if your parent will be back tonight.

The Change You Want is Within You

You who may sometimes have to be put up?
As the rent has not been paid
Or urged you to 'tell the teacher you are orphaned!'
Where's your parent since the last drinking spree?

For you women with black eyes due to last night's 'accident!'
You men too ashamed to shout or cry as it's not cultural
This is for you vulnerable children not safe in your house
For you who feel blamed for just being you

Anyone too challenged to move and have to keep it all in
How do we redeem ourselves and those after us?
This is for all of us who choose to stand up for change.
This is to all of us!

It wasn't long before Mellie's third daughter was born. How could she give a baby girl to an African man who inwardly expected a proper heir? It was a child but not a son! Fredrick resented her for being a girl. She was born in June 1948 just as the rainy season was subsiding. Guest was her name. She was 'the long-awaited visitor'. She was like Mellie in every way. She had a soft heart, was compassionate and did not like to see others suffer. She kept to herself. Many years later when her husband died early she kept to herself. She would not bother asking for help. She cried easily when she experienced pain. She was always motherly to her young siblings and they found her company easy. She was slow to challenge, had a leap of hearty laughter and swore by the donkey's rights - "I swear by the donkey." - A refrain she used often to stop herself from swearing.

After Guest came another girl. Her name was Guy. Tough as leather. She grew up to feel as if life treated her unfairly. She didn't associate much with the rest of her family. It was as if she looked down on them as ones who had easy lives and did not know what it was to suffer.

She was tall and beautiful and very nice when she was in a good mood. She was generous and expected the recipient to realize how hard she had worked to provide. She was a good worker, an achiever and highly gifted in handicraft.

The next two children, Mulili and Loki, were also successfully brought into this world. Mellie had two daughters and two sons. Life began to return to normal. Fredrick, who still experienced moments of drunkenness lived and worked in Nairobi for much of the year, coming back on weekends for visits. Mellie was left to her own devices to look after her children and her land

Fredrick did well at his job and slowly began to move up the corporate ladder. As he did, his money increased. As his money increased, so did the drink and the brief moments of drunkenness begun to grow. One bottle turned into two, which turned into four. Eventually, their doctor in Nairobi warned him against the drink, telling him that it had affected his liver. Had he indications of liver cirrhosis? He had to undergo an operation and was told he risked severe liver damage if he ever drank again.

Something serious was looming. Several years later, while his children were still in primary school, he lost his job because of the drink. Nobody knew then that he suffered addiction and that its name was alcoholism.

Having lost his job in the 1960s, he had no reason to stay in Nairobi and so he came home to Makueni, where he continued to 'oil' himself properly. He was gradually becoming more and more unpredictable.

Mellie was by now economically stable from farming and could cope for some time even without his salary. She had hoped they would work together to double their efforts to make excellent what she had managed on her own.

The education of his daughters began to irritate him. While it was not a priority, he felt somehow obliged to educate them at least for a few years. But those few years had now passed and the money spent on their education was something Fredrick wanted for himself.

'Why must they be educated further,' he thought to himself and sometimes said out loud. 'They already know all they need and they will not need more. When they are grown and married, this education will not help them. Their husbands will help them.' He never said this last part out loud in front of Mellie.

He was frustrated that he had to ask Mellie for money to maintain his lifestyle. So, he drank cheap brew at the 'witch's' den and the more he drank, the more violent he became to Mellie and the children. The alcohol would flood his brain and the quiet man would turn to a loud and angry bear.

Many times, he returned home drunk and caused unrest in his home. He would walk through the door stumbling and yelling. Swinging his arms around and trying to hit anything that moved. The children would run away into the forest and wait until he fell asleep before they could return to their rooms. He talked most of the night though.

Sometimes the family went to the neighbors' and he went after them searching everywhere; violence propelling him forward.

Mellie and her children spend their lives in the heart of darkness not knowing where their father and husband would turn up next. For the children, it was particularly difficult if the next day was a school day. After a night of running and escaping into the forest, how could anyone expect them to concentrate in class or even keep their eyes open? Tiredness grew and their perpetually red eyes began to develop bags underneath them.

They were always on high alert. Their senses were well attuned and highly focused in case they heard, smelt, or saw him. More often than not they would hear or smell him before they saw him. The drink made him loud and his entire being stank of alcohol. The home was no longer a place to belong, to feel loved and valued. It was rather a war zone when their father was around and it was a ticking time bomb when he was not; for sooner or later he would show up. His loud voice would be heard way off and his silhouette would appear in the doorway. Then it would be time again to take to their heels.

Life was one long race.

In the days of occasional drunkenness, it was simply yelling and confusion. Mellie could usually calm him down by not saying a word back to him. But now there was true fear. There was no hope of coming within striking range of him. Fredrick had a sharpened machete that nobody else would touch. Its edge glistened where the blade had been sharpened, its smooth edge interrupted with small cuts caused by the blacksmith's stone. This was the weapon, his weapon, which he would use to threaten his family. He would swear and stumble about, swinging it with terrible aim but dangerous effect.

So, they ran, always they ran. They ran to the forest; they ran to the neighbors. Wherever he was not, they ran. For how could they stand up to him? One night, Fredrick came into the house carrying a knife. It was not his usual machete. It was shorter, like a dagger. He chased the family from the house with surprising speed for a drunk man. Guest ran through the forest to the neighbor's house. When she reached the front of the house the neighbor was there and Guest ran up to her and buried herself in her arms for protection. Her name was Naomi and she was tall and strongly built.

"Shhh!" she whistled through the gap between her top front teeth. Naomi calmed Guest as best as she could. "Let us sit out in the stars, for when does he come here?"

So, Guest and the neighbor began to calm down as they huddled together in the cool of the night, looking up and wondering as to the path of their lives. Naomi was beautiful. She was the third and most beloved wife of her husband. She was a hardworking farmer and a good cook. There was always food in the house and she offered some to Guest that night. Guest simply shook her head, knowing getting food would mean departing from the arms of this woman. The fear she had surpassed hunger. The neighbor was right, Fredrick rarely ever came down to the neighbors' in pursuit of his family. He had a little respect for this woman for she could stand up to him. But tonight, Fredrick did not stop his pursuit, he did not change target. Despite his drunkenness, he walked stealthily to where the neighbor and his daughter were seated under the starry night sky. He crept from behind the house, slowly. Each step brought him closer to the two who were sitting calming down trying to forget what was happening. Naomi was warming herself in the dying charcoal fire as it was a cool evening. They were illuminated by the moonlight. The fire that burned since the dusk was not out. It was smoking slightly and casting the tiniest golden glow.

The wind blew softly over their faces as they sat upwind of Fredrick's creeping body. Did they smell something? The wind changed direction.

He crept forward in the night. As he turned the corner to see them, he slashed in the air with the knife, meaning to cut off his daughter's neck. But he was drunk and despite the stealthy ambush, his aim was still untrue. Guest was tethered to the spot. Her instinct told her to raise her arm to defend herself. She screamed silently. Her hand connected with the knife and it slit her palm open.

For a second Guest was stunned until she felt the warmth of the blood against her forearm as it ran down and dripped onto her feet. Her father was stabilizing his feet to attack again. She jumped up and ran into the forest, disappearing into the darkness. He ran after her. But a drunk, a grown man cannot keep the speed of a small child through a dense growth of leaves and plants. Whatever stealth, speed and cunning Fredrick had used to follow her thus far had evaporated after the adrenaline rush of the attempted murder. She continued to run as fast as she could. Each time she tripped, she righted herself, ignoring the pain.

Eventually, he gave up. Naomi ran into the forest to find her. She called in whisper "child, it is I, Naomi. Come out please, your father has left." There was no response.

Guest was not found until the early hours of the next morning, exhausted and drained of much blood. She could hardly stand and collapsed into the arms of her neighbor. It was lucky she was found at all for the jungle is not a place to lose one's way not to mention the deadly snakes! And finding a child within the jungle anyway.

Luckily, the dagger did not slice through any important arteries or veins. Guest would later say about her father in his old age, "I wish in all my life I had the courage to ask him to pay me back for the blood I lost that night!" She also wished she could ask the question no one knew the answer to.

"Why on earth did he want to kill me?"

Whatever the reason, she appreciated being spared.

Before she turned fourteen, life became so unbearable that she decided she would rather be married than spend her life running. When she was dancing one evening at the local village dance she met a fellow named Baraka, meaning Blessing. He too loved to dance. It was here dancing under the dim hurricane lamp, in the full moonlight and the African starry night sky and the lively Kamba music that they fell in love. Baraka liked to wear bell-bottom trousers and long-sleeved tight shirts. It was the fashion at the time, as was his hairstyle of a medium-cut up top and a line cut on the right side. He smoked cigarettes and weed and he traded bhang to subsidize his income which he got from working in the city.

So, Guest got married and did not come back for many years. She remained loyal to Baraka and Baraka to her until his premature death due to a road accident many years later. Though it seemed unimaginable that she would go on to mother seven children and be happy, more or less. None of this, however, would be known to Mellie for some time.

Meanwhile, the rest of the family continued running. When the sun fell, they ran and during the night, they hid. Like a wounded lion, he chased after them and like weak, scared antelopes, they never stood in one spot for too long. Mellie once said, "I used to spend the whole day with hungry children, uprooting trees and stumps from people's farms in order to get money to buy food. If he came as the food was cooking, he would lift the pot and throw it out of the house. Tired and hungry we all dispersed." Mellie would then spend the night tracking her children down. It was something she would get very used to doing over the years. They no longer knew what plenty or even enough was.

There was a gap in time before a sixth child came and it was a girl. Nduku was her name. She died after birth, the umbilical cord wrapped around her neck, too tired to even make her first cry.

In no time, Ally was born and he was the storyteller. He used to kid everyone. He would disguise his voice and chat with a neighbor like he was a fellow woman friend of hers, he would engage in conversation from outside her house and she inside.

"Hodi," he would say. "How are you this morning Mama Yoni?"

She would respond "Let me come out...we are good and everyone is good this morning."

"Ah, it is fine. Do not worry about leaving your house. You are busy and we can talk here. Tell me some news."

Like this, Ally would try to keep the conversation going as long as possible until, upon coming out of the house, his conversation partner would discover that she had been talking all the time with Ally. He was the family clown.

The land Fredrick bought was the land on which they now lived, it was land bought during a time of plenty. It was a good stretch of land, sloping westerly and sitting alongside the biggest river flowing through the area. It was perfect for both crop and animal farming and Mellie worked hard to ensure the land bent to her will. It was prosperous and giving.

Fredrick did not work the land. When he lost his job and moved out of the city. He decided not to work again and just to drink. As he drunk, the money he had with him began to dwindle. While fertile land lay within his grasp, the drinking was too strong and as the drinking continued, the money decreased.

Mellie only heard of the buyer when he and his associates came to view the land. Their neighbor, a man named Tiso, saw Mellie's land and wanted it for himself. He knew Fredrick liked the drink and he knew Fredrick had no job. So, his wife made a brew and allowed Fredrick to drink it, not asking him to pay but allowing him to build up credit. He drank and drank for weeks, unburdened by the worries of how he would eventually pay.

When finally, payment was demanded, Fredrick was blindsided and he ordered Mellie to march the cattle to the nearest market and sell them. All the cattle were sold but this was not enough. So Tiso and his wife suggested payment in land exchange. Surely Fredrick had not built up credit enough to have to pay in form of land!

It was the word of a drunkard against the crafty neighbors.

Mellie could prove nothing. But she could go to the chief of the area. The chief's camp was three kilometers away, at the Convenient Centre where the colonial masters met the people to make any major announcement. When she arrived, she met with the chief and pleaded with him to stop the sale of the land. She said, "I'm married to Fredrick and I have five children. I would like to ask you to stop him from proceeding with the sale of our land."

The chief listened and was moved. But the clerk who was his confidant and also a distant cousin of Fredrick's was not. He went to the chief and said "Bwana chief if a man owns a shirt he has a right to do as he wills with it. What this woman says is nonsense."

Mellie knew enough English to pick up a few words, including the words "No sense". This was a word she would never forget all her life. The chief listened to his advisor and did not stop the sale of the land. She was sent home. She picked her sisal 'kiondo' (basket) and dragged her heavy feet helplessly out of that office.

So, Fredrick sold his land and his cattle in order to pay for the drink (which he had already taken). That was the day they became as poor as church mice.

After they lost their land, Fredrick disappeared for some time and went back to his father's house. Mellie found work and a place to stay in a local settlement scheme in the district, working for some of her distant kin. No human had ever settled there before but it was somewhere they could stay and beggars cannot be choosers. All Mellie had to do was work on the farm. At this settlement, she was even given a small place to build a makeshift house, though it never really became home. The only evidence that remained of their good life was this three- bedroomed house. She passed by her former land and shed tears every time. She would shake her head and wonder who would ever have guessed she would once be homeless. Each morning, as early as she could, Mellie would rise leaving Fredrick in their now hut to sleep in. She would step outside and stretch, looking out to the river which ran several hundred meters away from them. This river was a constant reminder of her home because she now lived across the same river, poor and a squatter. Then she would report for duty. Mellie knew that this was a long fall from her previous life. Previously these menial jobs would have been done by someone in a lower class than Mellie. But the money was gone and she had no choice. If only her husband would work with her, they would still have a good life!

She had to be ready before the sun got too hot. She would then work till evening. The farms, which were up to twenty acres, were recently cleared of their trees and all that remained was their stumps. These stumps made it impossible for the oxen to plough the fields properly without risking injury. Mellie's job was to change that.

Whenever she approached a new tree, Mellie's special hoe would be lifted above her head. The skill learned from childhood was to split the wood into smaller pieces to allow them to be lifted from the earth. Standing on the tree stump itself was the most effective but most dangerous. One wrong swing could cut an ankle or send the wielder flying.

Mellie never swung wrong.

Even working tirelessly, she only managed to pull out a few stumps a day. Her hands developed blisters and bruises but she did not complain. Some days she was blessed to come across stumps whose roots were dry or rotten, making them easier to remove. Some days it rained and the roots were easier to extract.

Being of distant kin was more a curse than a blessing and Mellie found her employers to be some of the worst payers she knew. Her wage was given in broken instalments and much of it was never given. But she needed the money.

Mellie was a Christian woman and she believed she worked for God, not just her employers. So, she would go back, no matter how difficult the work was or how little the pay. Each morning she would enter the compound, a hoe on her shoulder, a wrap around her waist and rosary beads in her hand.

"Good morning," she would declare once she had met her employer some meters from their house. She would usually address the person by their relationship name – such as 'my uncle's daughter' – or by their tribe name. "Do you need any casual laborers?"

"Not really," was almost always the response but Mellie knew she could get there with a little push.

"I can see your beans need weeding before they flower. I have nothing to cook for my children tonight so let me weed for them."

"My husband won't come till the end of the month so I have no money to give you."

"Can you pay me in kind? Maybe give me some food to cook tonight?"

It was the only way to ensure she worked, but Mellie knew that the longer she negotiated, the lower the deal went and she would end up out of desperation doing more than she got paid for. And when the kin's husband did end up coming home, she was never given all that she was owed. Her main survival technique was to work till evening, until the people she worked for were eating and then pass by the house, asking either to be paid in kind or to receive her wages. Sometimes it worked but usually if she received food it was old, off or scraps.

But Mellie was a fighter and had the resilience of a tank. She continued to do casual jobs in farms. Sometimes walking far before she found someone willing to employ her. But she always found work to be done. Like a tractor, she worked on people's farms. She needed their money more than they needed her labor. She weeded their vast plots of land for peanut wages, but she was highly grateful.

The real danger was the snakes and scorpions that hid in the dirt. Most of the adult snakes would slither away when they heard her coming, but the younger ones, the ones more prone to attack, would not know to run. They would stay there until unearthed. If they bit, there was no telling how much venom was injected into the body. Baby snakes were very dangerous.

It was an incredible thing to see an experienced field worker uncover a snake. The hoe would flip the earth, revealing the snake and causing the worker to jump back. Always alert to such dangers and always ready, the hoe in a single and smooth motion would be swung around high over the head and sent crashing down onto the head of the still-disorientated snake, decapitating it. This was harder to do with scorpions, given their smaller size, but it could sometimes still be done.

Before she started working, she would pray for protection and for the will to work well. The children would have their mouths agape when she showed them the area she had to work. Especially Ally, who often had to accompany her during her work. He would ask "Mother, where have you to work up to before we can go home?"

She would say, "Son, it will not be long before we will be on our way. Just sit there and before you know it I will be finished. It's only up to that tree over there. Sit there and tell me some of the stories narrated in school."

She would then start to work stopping occasionally to chew her tobacco and drink some water under the shade of the jacaranda tree.

When Ally came with her he would plead, "Mum, it is nearly three o'clock, the midday plane already passed long ago," (There was a plane that always flew over at exactly noon a regular mark that it was nearly lunchtime) "please mom, and can we go home now?"

"My son, sit under that shade and let me finish just this bit."

Sometimes he waited and waited. He was not only tired but hungry. The water they had carried was tasteless. Eventually, for he knew his mother was scared of leopards he hatched a plan.

"Mum, I just heard some movement in the forest behind me. I say it is a leopard!" He jumped up and ran towards her calling for help, "mum!" She took the bait and they ran like hares and went home. Whenever he wanted to go home, he used that trick and it always worked with his mother. He did not realize it, but it also meant they did not get paid and they did not get food.

She spent many whole hot days working on an empty stomach.

This suffering she underwent changed the way she treated casual laborers working in her home many years later. She strongly believed that if anyone came to do any work, they were to be properly fed. She said, "If a casual worker is not fed in my home, I will take my own portion and give it to them. I know how it feels like to work without food and I will not like any woman's child to go through a similar experience." During this time, Fredrick came and went. When he went, he wasn't missed and when he came, Mellie welcomed him as she believed a wife should. He was, after all, still her husband. This is was culturally and religiously expected of her.

Reflection time

What do you do when you feel threatened by an empowered wife?

How can a gentleman empower himself so that he supports and loves his family?

Culturally men and women had places where they could be counselled. Those circles are weak or no longer there. Healing workshops are great places where nowadays people can find a space to talk and be listened to as they disentangle from self-defeating behavior.

There could have been a cultural aspect to the violence in which corporal punishment was used on women and children by men. When this happened, in some cases, the women believed that it was out of 'love'. I want to believe the reader will realize that and especially those who are survivors of violence that it does affect those who witness or even receive it. The challenge is for those who experience anger to look for less harmful ways to discipline. I want to believe that getting help is one way someone can learn alternative ways of dealing with anger so that children and others learn by being differently mentored rather than through violence.

I also believe strongly that the cycle of violence can be broken so that members of a family get to talk about issues as they happen. Too often there is a silence behind physical violence, even an untold silence behind verbal violence. What is behind the silence or the many words?

What do you want your partner to do?

What do you need from her or him?

Deep within we want to be loved by and to love people we deeply care about. So, let us find solutions together to navigate this new terrain of finding new ways to be family.

~CHAPTER FIVE~
HARD TIMES PASS.

Many women share economic disempowerment is one reason they stay in abusive relationships; made all the more intense when they have children. In these situations, resources are a problem especially when the core source of livelihood is shaken.

Women being jobless and again the expectations to adhere to the cultural roles as in Mellie's case only to be a housewife makes provision a challenge. What happens when men lose jobs? Could they cope differently with the stress? One wonders if the domestic violence was activated by the fact that Fredrick felt out of control when Mellie became economically empowered. The question, however, is how empowerment can be viewed as 'with' each other rather than 'against' each other? How can resources be used to enhance happiness in the family no matter how little they are? Maybe the issues are deeper than resources.

How can fathers and husbands act as a buffer for their wives and children?

Children in violent situations need a lot of understanding from adults who handle them in other institutions. The children from violent homes experience debilitating fear which can affect their lives unless helped to talk about what they are going through. Nowadays, teachers and others are more equipped with the skills to handle children with care. I have found equipping children with skills to help them cope with difficult domestic situations helps in bringing out the best in them and helping to break the cycle of violence even if only for themselves.

Non-violence begins with each individual, with each of us whether it is in our attitudes, thoughts, behavior or otherwise.

As time went on, life moved into what, for Mellie, held a semblance of normalcy. Mato was born. He had a good appetite. He breastfed very well and became a very strong boy. No wonder he got to like cooking so much. He cooked mostly and at rare times Ally helped. Mellie cooked at Christmas and at big feasts. She would sit on her stool and work. (This was a special stool that was carved and given to a Kamba woman when she got married. It was smooth like a milk gourd).

Mato was a very loving brother. He was the one who Baby would get to know best. Baby was to be Mellie's final child. She wouldn't come into the world until years later and she wouldn't really get to know Mato until several years after that. In her later years, she would remember one time before she had started school; she found him cutting unripe pawpaw with a very sharp knife. Before he knew it, she was next to him. She was fascinated by the way it cut so neatly ta ta ta! "Let me hold it for you, Mato". Before he could reply, the knife had come down and cut through the pawpaw to her middle finger on her little right hand. She pulled it and cried for the rest of that day. They were both shocked. 'Baby, sorry! Sorry! Sorry! Let me see.' He pleaded. Baby would not let him examine it. Upon seeing the blood, she was sure she was going to die. This is what blood meant! The pain she felt! She could still feel the sharp knife going through. She held it tight in the heart of her other hand. Then Mato said sorry again and promised to give her his share of the yellow scones and juice famously known then as 'Treetop' when mother came home. The finger never healed properly from the cut, leaving a rough scar for the rest of her life and a slight sensation whenever she fully stretched out her hand.

After that day, Mato was the first aider in the family. He always had a kit consisting of some methylated spirit, cotton, a pair of scissors, some iodine, bandages and other simple items in case someone had a cut or a burn. He was kind and he liked to attend to people's needs.

Mellie was always a woman of faith and this enabled her to believe in providence all throughout her life. She believed that even if she did not have means today God would always show some light at the end of the tunnel. It was not easy. At difficult times when she felt someone was taking advantage of her, she compared them to those who chew stones with other people's teeth and do not know how it feels like. This was especially relevant when her employer treated her like trash, sending her home with no pay after she had done a day's work. Her children learned to value work early in life from seeing their mother go through such hardship.

In order to continue working Mellie and her family occasionally had to move from one farm to another though never far away from each other. They lived from relative to relative, semi-nomadically, always staying as long as there was work or as long as they were allowed.

Once they were old enough, Mulili and Loki left home and went to herd animals. At least that way they could get food and shelter. And they were away from the unpredictable violence of their father. Guy too left, but she left when the money ran out and Mellie could no longer afford to send her to school. Nobody knew for some time exactly what became of her. In time, they learned that, like Guest, to whom Mellie had kept somewhat in contact, she had found someone who would love her. She had gotten married. In fact, it was to Guest that Guy first ran and Guest had tried to help. But Guy was strong-willed and unmoved from the path she decided to walk. She left Guest's house shortly after arriving and disappeared again. It would be some time before she was seen again and any information about the life she had led or the man she had married remained as secret as those years she was away.

Now it was just Mellie, Mato and Ally.

Versus Fredrick. It is said that the darkest hour is just before dawn. One evening Fredrick came home. He had been drinking for some time and as Mellie and her children had just moved he had some trouble finding them. When he did he was still intoxicated and he became very, very wild; wilder than Mellie had ever seen. It was suppertime but the pot of food was over the fire boiling away. Fredrick grabbed it not feeling the burn and tried to throw it over, Mellie. Luckily she was quick and she moved out of its way. He dropped the clay pot breaking it into pieces scattering the contents in and kicked the fire sending embers everywhere.

The children's eyes wet with despair after a long day of waiting for a meal! Mellie could see in his eyes a murderous rage she hadn't seen before. She could see he was thirsting for her blood.

She looked at her two children and back at Fredrick. He had turned and was advancing towards her. As he stepped forward, his foot went into another pot and he stumbled and fell. This was Mellie's chance. Mellie grabbed her children, one in each arm and fled. Into the jungle, hearing Fredrick closing the distance, she ran, counting on him to not know this jungle as she did. It took some time but finally, his yells of drunken rage got further and further until they disappeared altogether. But Mellie did not stop running. She had learned all those years ago, that Fredrick could be sneaky. He had after all attacked Guest at their old neighbor's house. Mellie dared not stop. He could be sneaky, but he could not be quick. If Mellie kept moving she would be safe. With Mato now on her back and Ally in tow, she ran.

This time she did not come back. As soon as she could, she left Ally with her relatives, safe from the reach of Fredrick. Ally was too small to travel unsupervised and Mellie could not carry him. Only Mato remained with her now. She did not cry as she said goodbye for she had a journey ahead and tears were energy she could not afford to waste.

During the day she travelled. The first day she caught the only bus in the area. Every second day one bus left the village, travelling one day and then returning the next. Luck had favored Mellie for the bus was departing this morning.

She travelled as far as she dared on the bus before getting off to walk the rest of the way to her unknown destination. When she stepped onto the dirt she counted her belongings. There was no more money. She had used it to pay for her bus, planning to travel further but ultimately fearing the prying eyes of everyone around her.

She lifted her baby onto her back and tied him there using her flowery kanga. "My child, the safari has now started. We have to get past that hill over there. Kiima Kiu, the Black Hill."

Mato, of course, understood none of this but Mellie was talking to herself as much as she was to him.

The bus had driven through most of the forty-two horseshoe corners of Makongo, up and down the hilly landscape. But the biggest and highest of hills was still in front of Mellie. She looked up at the bright afternoon sun. Two o'clock more or less. The sun here was consistent, rising and setting around six in the morning and evening. It didn't take much to learn how to guess the time from looking up at the sky.

While the snaking roads offered smooth walking, being too long on them greatened her risk of being found. So most of the journey was across the jungle and forest lands. As Mellie stepped off the earthen road her canvas shoes winced as they came into contact with the barren ground. They were smooth at the soles and barely there. Mellie's feet felt every pebble, every branch and every thorn.

Mellie was atop the second to last steep hill that she would have to climb. Ahead of her in the distance was the Black Hill but before she could make it there she would have to descend this one. Every ounce of her had to focus on not falling as the steep descent began. To her right, the bus had left, driving slowly out of shot. Soon it would bend around another horseshoe and come back, winding its way down the hill. Mellie's direct approach would out speed the bus, though the bus didn't have to worry about tumbling down the hill.

Mellie grabbed every tree, root and branch as she made her descent. With her son on her back, she keenly steadied her knees and selectively stepped on the firm rocks. She avoided looking too far ahead in case she got dizzy. With a slowly dehydrated and hungry child on her back, this was the quickest and best way to her destination, wherever that was.

As she thought of the child on her back, the others came to mind. Where were they? Were they alive? Her pace began to slow. No! Mellie emptied her mind. She could think of nothing but the journey, nothing but her next stop. She needed to find somewhere she could stay and somewhere she could eat. She hadn't eaten since the day before.

Her foot slipped on a detached branch and Mellie fell. Her hand tightened around the root she was holding and her bottom took the fall. She grimaced and began to swear before changing her mind and pleading for help from Our Lady.

"Mary Mother of Mercy, help me and my child."

She checked that her son was alright. A little shocked but unhurt, Mato remained relatively oblivious to the trials that were upon him. Mellie remained seated long enough to reach for some tobacco she was carrying. Chewing it sharpened her mind.

She kept walking down the valley. The hours crept on. By the time she came to the bottom the first signs of dusk were surfacing. As she approached the bottom of the hill, there was evidence of a river with huge, green trees found only in places with underground rivers. But she couldn't see any water. She was dehydrated and she needed to drink badly. This area was deserted and she needed to climb out before darkness fell. She walked up the bed and found a path to climb from the valley. It was badly eroded with bare rocks and branches scattered loosely she could easily tell it was a track people used to climb from the valley. She kept climbing.

Suddenly the sound of bells broke the silence of Mellie's panting breath. It was the sound of mission bells.

"It is six o'clock, my son. That is the bell for the Angelus."

Making the sign of the cross she began to pray in her mind. She could do this. When she had finished the prayer, her tired legs walked a little faster. She still had a few kilometers to cover and dusk was approaching fast. She passed some herds of cattle as they were coming home from grazing.

After the sun hit the horizon, it took only half an hour for the land to go completely black. Just before this time, with the tiniest of rays of the sun still peeking over the edge of the earth, Mellie saw the cross on top of the mission building. She could hear voices.

Mato had fallen asleep from exhaustion and hunger.

She saw the gate of the church. She stopped, made the sign of the cross and was grateful God had brought her this far. Then she entered, seeking shelter for the night.

The thin soles of her shoes were now riddled with holes.

The next day her journey continued. It would take a few days before she would cross the Black Hill. After that, who knew? All she had to do was keep going. During the days she walked when she could and she sought shelter from the hot sun when her child could take the heat no longer. During the night she stopped at people's homes if she could. In this scarcely populated land, connections were made by saying what clan one originated from. For many years, people were prohibited from marrying from the same clan because they were seen as sisters and brothers. And so, if Fredrick's father came from one clan, the wife, or wives, had to come from a different clan. Therefore, when strangers met introductions would consist of the name of the person followed by the father's clan and the mother's clan. That way, both people would somehow find a point of connection, even if it was as far up as their grandfather's wife's clan.

In this way, strangers would become family and hospitality was always given to a family. Mellie managed to survive the nights through these encounters, though she would still have to toil in the farm for a few hours the next day to pay back the goodness given to her before she continued her journey.

In the end Mellie made it to her sister in-law's house. She was washed out and needed food and a place to sleep. The baby on her back, her seventh child, had sucked all the milk and she felt like it was sucking blood. Mellie explained to the sister-in-law what was going on with her husband, that she had no place to stay with the children, that she had now come to the end of her tether and had left him. She begged and pleaded, asking for a place to stay and food to eat. But she had forgotten that blood was thicker than water and her sister-in-law would not help her. Mellie pleaded more. Eventually, the sister-in-law relented and Mellie was sent to share the night with the chicken and the goats.

That was a long night for Mellie and her child sitting there in the barn made of wound-together trees for walls and a grass-thatched roof. In here the wind could easily enter and the warmth could easily escape. The hard and rocky floor interspersed with hay and bird feed and faeces was no bed. All kinds of pests were here, including mites and ticks and spiders. Was that a creeping creature, prowling around Mellie and her child? Goat pee drenched the barn dispelling it of oxygen. The smell was a killer. In spite of her being deadbeat, she hardly closed her eyes. What a long night before dawn?

"Imagine spending a night with a baby in such a place. I will never ever forget as long as I live." She said out loud to nobody, for there was nobody to tell it to.

She had spent the whole night interceding through 'Our Lady'.

"Hail Mary full of grace.... Please help me know what to do. I don't know what to do in this situation. Show me some light".

She then remembered she had been saying her rosary and continued ... "Pray for us sinners, now and at the hour of our death. Amen."

She consistently squeezed bead after bead till morning broke. She left silently early the next morning for a destination unknown to her, surviving like before, eating if she could and toiling in the fields to pay for her night's rest. She walked for weeks in total, telling nobody where she was going. How could she? She didn't know where she was going. And even if she did, she did not want anyone to know in case they broke the news to her husband, who was presumably still hunting her.

Her parents-in-law had died and her sister Malia had married far away. Who was she to turn to? She thought of her godmother, Telesia. Maybe she would put Mellie up for some time before deciding what to do next. She walked and walked for days, over the hills and down the valleys till she got to her godmother whom she had not seen since her teenage years. She was a strong and tough woman but this journey was more than she had ever done before, more than the hours ploughing the fields, more than the unending number of trees she had uprooted, more than any of the work she had done. If she could survive this she would be set to take on any challenge that faced her.

If she could survive.

When she got closer to her destination she realized she didn't know where the house was, so she went to the local parish to get directions, for she knew her godmother was a well-known parishioner. By the time she was nearing the parish, she was weather-beaten. She dragged her lead-heavy feet, blistered and burning through the thick calluses' life had built up for her. She had walked so long that stopping made her feet sear with pain. When she wiped her face, her hand had white crystals from dehydration. Her lips were as dry as dust and they cracked. She felt like she would lose her mind from thirst. A figure began walking towards her, blurry as a mirage.

"Ah! Dear Jesus and His holy mother! Is this you Mellie, my child?"

It was Telesia. Mellie's heart leapt if that was still a possible exertion of energy. Her godmother continued, "What a pleasant surprise! I have been thinking about you lately and then God brings you to me. Welcome my daughter. Sit down and tell me all about yourself."

Mellie was led into a quiet room in the parish. When she sat, she winced as the pain in her feet flared up before subsiding into a manageable ache. Her godmother waited patiently, for she could see that whatever had happened to Mellie was intense and would soon be revealed to her. Mellie was given water to drink and some food to eat. Her godmother waited.

The reunion was electrifying. The two women connected on a heart to heart level that Mellie had not experienced in a long time. The room was like a confessional box, listening without judging as Mellie and Telesia talked. There they sat for most of the night as each shared in the effect of elapsed time, updating and reliving each of their lives.

It was here that Mellie's life began to change. In that parish, there was a missionary priest. Her godmother advised her, "Sure, you have nothing to lose by telling him your story." Mellie considered it and decided to try. She pleaded with this Holy Ghost Missionary to give her a job.

She started, "I have six children and I'm wedded in the church and my husband has turned violent and wants to kill us all. I have been doing manual jobs to provide for the family. My husband has sold our land and cattle. Whenever he is told I have been seen in a particular place, he comes to get me. I've walked for weeks to get here as I've nowhere else to go. If I do not get any job, my children will die. Actually, I do not know where some of my children are and neither do they know where I am. I have one desire – to get my family together and be able to feed them."

At this, she blinked to keep back tears but it was too late. She broke down and her river of pain began to flow. She had kept it together for so long and the dam which was holding it back broke with a force she could not remember feeling before. It was the only way she could keep going – by looking and being strong. She could not remember ever before opening her soul to anyone who just listened and listened. She could feel her heart threatening to break free from her ribcage. She wished aloud that she could reverse her motherhood. "I sometimes wish I could 'swallow' these children! That way they would be free from this life of pain."

Her suffering was heart-breaking and dehumanizing. The priest simply listened and took in her story. His softened heart was seen in the change in his eyes as he heard and felt all the pain that Mellie had gone through. When she was finished he thought for a few moments and eventually told her to go see Friar Kablack. He could get her a job, though it wouldn't be a particularly glamourous one.

Mellie was grateful. She could not believe what she had heard the friar say. Her heart beat a little faster but this time with joy of expectation. She did not mind. It was a job and that was all she needed. All agreed it was the foundation by which Mellie could begin to rebuild her life. She was able to find joy in any kind of job for she was hardworking and devoted.

Reflection Time: hard times pass.

When we do not stay conscious and aware of our feelings or what happens to us when we experience others and life, then, we may be choosing to repeat what has been done to us. I want to encourage you to know that there is the hope of behavior change even when we have observed and experienced violence.

I would like to invite you to imagine you are in a very safe place. Imagine and create your space and make it as safe as you can. Maybe you imagine surrounded by people you love and who value you. Feel this safety for a little longer. Feel your breath getting long and deep. Feel your body becoming warm and relaxed. Your heart rate has slowed down as you feel safe and loved.

Remember that: You do not do anything that deserves violence.
Violence affects us and others.
We can learn new ways of being with each other.

~CHAPTER SIX~
JOB, GLORIOUS JOB...

What are you grateful for in your life right now? See if even in the midst of all that is happening you can create time to notice the blessings.

When Mellie got the job, she only knew the whereabouts of two out of six of her children. She informed her employer about her five other children and that she did not know where four of them were – for she knew where Ally was and Mato was with her. She knew they were not in school. Before beginning her job and starting her new life, her employer allowed her to hunt down her children. Presumably, they were roughly in the same area.

Leaving Mato in the care of her godmother, Mellie ventured forth. She began by going back to her brother's home. The return journey was not as long or as tedious as the one before as she was given some small money for the buses. She had a bounce in her steps and confidence as she walked straight. The last time she had felt this sense of purpose was when she was newly married. For some reason, she no longer feared – or she no longer cared – being discovered by Fredrick. Either way, he would not be searching along this route.

It still took her a few days on the slow buses but when she arrived she discovered that Guy, her second daughter had eloped. Rather than spending the nights outside and miserable, she opted for the lesser evil – marriage. This way at least she could sleep peacefully and settle into a routine, rather than spend her life fighting to survive.

During Mellie's time, tribes lived in specific areas, occupying the land of around seventy kilometers in radius. To leave this area and go where they did not speak their language was too great a risk for Mellie's lost children. So, she thought they would be somewhere in this area.

Because relationships were tracked through clan and lineage and Mellie knew her children could only really get jobs as herders, she knew where and how to look. She walked many kilometers long, searching here and there, asking for the aid of strangers.

"I am Mellie and I am looking for two youngsters aged between seven and fourteen. Could you have seen or got word about such children? The bigger one is Mulili and both resemble each other very much."

This she would ask and if she received a negative response she would move on and ask the next. Finally, one day she asked a home owner this. He called to the local herdsman to see if the herdsman knew. The herdsman was an elderly man who was off duty and relaxing in the sunshine. His age and demeanor showed he had been herding for years and if these children were anywhere near, he would know. "Kiatu, come here. Have you seen any new boys herding in the neighborhood? The two are aged 7 and 14?"

Kiatu looked into the space above him in an attempt to remember. "They were not herding, but about a month ago I saw two boys playing a polythene ball at the river. They were about the age you speak of and both in tatters. But I'm afraid I haven't seen them since that day."

Mellie wasn't sure if she should hope or despair. A month was a long time, yet they couldn't get that far.

Kiatu interrupted her thought. "Follow this murram road," he pointed the way to a road which ran some way into the distance. "After that stony hill, there is a school on the right. Next to it, there is an iron thatched house and a bougainvillea tree with purple flowers at the gate. Go and enquire from there. They may know."

Mellie thanked them and continued with her journey. As she walked along she kept asking anybody walking past her about the duo. But nobody knew any more than the herdsman had already told her. Before the hill lay a seasonal river where the animals drank. Some boys were playing by the riverbed and her heart jumped. The closer she moved towards them the more they looked unfamiliar to her. Anyhow, she still asked these boys but they did not know. Maybe they had seen them some time ago but they were not sure.

Mellie continued. At least she was going in the right direction.

As she walked, her feet burned in the afternoon sun. She had shoes with thin soles for the only other pair she owned had been destroyed by her previous walk. When she arrived at the house with the purple flowers at the gate she began to walk towards it but the dogs barked wildly and she stopped.

"Are the owners in?" She shouted loudly so someone in the house could hear. She was afraid of dogs for she had once been attacked by a dog with rabies in one of her escapes.

There was no response. She shouted again. The dogs continued to bark. Her hands were getting wet with sweat. She slowly began to take tiny steps backwards while keeping an eye on the dogs. This was a tactic she had learnt in regard to wild animals – as much as possible you did not show them your back. Just then, the face of a boy popped out from behind a nearby tree. It was so covered in dust that only the whites of the eyes shone in the sun.

Mellie called again.

The boy recognized the voice and turned around, disappearing momentarily to shout "Mulili! Mulili! Come here! Mother is here!" Then Loki reappeared and ran towards his mom and jumped into her arms.

A moment later, Mulili appeared in the distance, running. He too, almost ran through his mother as he embraced her. Mellie cried tears for joy. She had her sons back. But there were tears of sadness in her eyes as well. As she rubbed their back she felt their tiny bones! How thin they were. How in tatters. They had barely eaten.

By now, the owner had come out of the house, in shock. Mellie's mood was ecstatic but she calmed herself down to greet the homeowner and to explain the situation before continuing on her journey.

The clothes her children had on their backs were the same ones worn when they left home. They were nearly completely shredded. Both boys' hair was brown from malnourishment and their skin was pale and scaly. The size of their heads was exaggerated and their stomachs were bloated from lack of food. But they were over the moon, it could be seen in their bright eyes and their smiles were a sight to behold. This soothed Mellie's heart momentarily.

As Mulili and Loki held their mother's hands, each competed to tell their version of the story. Because they were herding they often didn't return till late in the evening and they were not guaranteed food. Like many other herding boys, they lived on wild fruit and small animals that they would hunt and roast as the animals grazed. Sometimes when hunger stung unbearably, they would milk the goats and take the milk raw while grazing.

"Mom, how did you know where we were?" Loki asked.

"My child, I never stopped praying for you since the day you ran away. Mary is the mother of mercy."

Mellie held back a tear and relished the thought: she had found her children.

It was a few hours journey to where Ally was but they made it with surprising speed, all pushed forward by the excitement of reuniting. Ally was young and so did not know the situation and why he was left there. When he saw his mother, he was happy and ran to her. Now her children were here. For Guest and Guy, she prayed. Life, she hoped, was treating them better than it did during the days of Fredrick.

At her relatives' house, Mellie and her children were all given food and, perhaps the biggest blessing of all, a car to take them back home! This was a great joy for Mellie and she said little, enjoying the immense blessing of not having to worry. As the crow flies her new home was not far but the crow flies over forests and other unconquerable lands. It would still take several days of walking and busing to reach if Mellie had to travel back. Who knew if she could make the journey with three of her children? Her journey of escape was a long, winding and unclear one and so it took many more weeks than it should have.

But all that was done now and Mellie could look to the future. When she brought them back she got them readmitted into primary school. They were as happy as larks to be back together. They completed their schooling and continued to secondary school. Mellie was able to pay for their education now that she was on a payroll. And things began to return to normal.

All the time that Mellie ran and during the day searched for her children, Fredrick hunted for her. But Mellie was blessed for though their neighbors knew little of where she was going and where her children were, what little they knew they didn't tell. They knew what kind of man Fredrick was and they weren't going to help him with his schemes.

So, Fredrick knew not what to do. And the more he searched but did not find, the angrier he got. He would go to his first-born daughter's home he thought. Guest might know. Guest had not returned since the day she ran away and eloped. She still held the scar along her palm and forearm where Fredrick had attacked her all those years ago.

Guest was living at home while her husband was in Nairobi. He had a good job and thus was afforded the opportunity to have a home here, sending money while he worked in the city. By the time Fredrick got to the house, it was already dark. He had thought that his wife was hiding there because he knew Guest and Mellie still kept in touch and that

Mellie had visited Guest before. He demanded that his daughter tell him where her mother was. When she said she had not seen her for ages, he did not believe her. His anger had reached a tipping point. He had come in drunk. He felt rage within him but he had no way to let it out. He looked for a knife but saw none. He shouted. As he left to go he saw the fire burning and slowly walked towards the kitchen.

Guest did nothing. As long as one is a child, one cannot stand up to a parent, especially an enraged drunk parent. And parents, especially fathers, should be respected. She remained stuck to her seat and watched Fredrick. Men did not enter kitchens for traditionally it was a woman's territory, but in he went breaking boundaries. She observed him bend to pick something from the hearth he did not smoke so what was he doing going to the fireplace? It was still.

Fredrick took a log from the fire and threw it on to the house, setting it ablaze. Then he left, the glow of the burning building in the background. Guest was for some few seconds glued to the ground, unable to believe her eyes, just blank. Then she blinked to reality and with a sudden rush of adrenaline sprang up to grab what she could in the seconds before the house was completely consumed. She ran to her husband who was in Nairobi. The house-made primarily of wood and mud went up in flames almost immediately and how could she make sense of this behavior? In Nairobi, she remained until enough money had been raised to rebuild their home.

According to the Kamba culture, a man cannot allow his sister and her husband to stay on his land. There are various reasons for this, one of which is to do with the expectation that men are providers enough for their family. When Fredrick was deemed incapable of taking care of his wife, it was incredibly degrading. He was despised for selling his land and then going on to ask to be put up in the same neighborhood. A man's family should not be dependent on other men.

So, when Mellie approached her stepbrother about staying with his family, he was hesitant. This was the brother to whom the bride price had been paid to, making the situation more complicated. A married woman cannot return to her parent's house for there are issues of inheritance and land ownership. As Mellie's father had died, this brother acted as her parents and so it was deemed inappropriate for her to return.

Her stepbrother was aware of what his sister had gone through but he was a man. He had responsibilities to his own family and bringing his sister together with her husband onto his land might not be deemed appropriate. She pleaded with him greatly and eventually he relented, showing her a plot of land far from the house on which to construct a semi-permanent house. This was on condition that her husband would never come to live on it. Mellie's husband could not be allowed to live on the land. Never.

Now that he had given her a place to live in, he expected her children to avail themselves to work whenever there was manual work on his farm. He would come to her house very early before dawn and call the children to go and plough his vast land. Whenever he got up before dawn, he wrapped his torso in his blanket and walked out in the cool morning. He stood in the middle of his farm and pointed to where the workers needed to till. He would say, "You weed beginning from that tree over there to that mango tree." This would be an area so large it would take them nearly three days to cultivate. Yet, he wanted it done in a day. Come evening he would pass by to evaluate.

Mellie's brother ran his home with an iron fist. He had a long whip which he used to beat his wives and children. He would ensure that everyone was working with the crack of that whip. Once, before Mellie arrived, there was a famine and the food stocks were running low. One of his wives went to him and reported there was no food for them. In his house he ate, even if the others went hungry. But they still needed some food so he went to the field and told his wife to take the skinniest cow he could see. He told her to sell it at the market for no less than five thousand shillings, an obscene price for a half-starved cow.

They could do nothing but obey. Whoever haggled at its price was turned back and went their way. All the other sellers sold their cows cheaper and were able to buy food for their families. Every week these women walked the long-distance until they tired of it, by which time the famine was over. Although the cow was saved, it took their families months to recover from the starvation they suffered in the famine. Despite the knowledge of this and the fear of the man with the whip, Mellie and her family had a home-like they had not had for several years now. They had a place they could sleep in peace.

Mellie was a good woman although her life had been one of pain caused largely by her husband. She lived in the hope that her husband would return to her. She still thought he would once more be a gentle and loving man. "God gave him to me. Maybe if I keep praying for him, he will be nice to me and treat me as when we first married". And she prayed for him. During their engagement and early marriage, he had been kind and endearing. She knew he was capable of being loving.

They had wedded in the Catholic Church and her conscience could not allow her to leave him. It was church law that couples stay together for better or worse. The church did not leave any leeway. Had the church ever imagined there actually was a 'worse' side of marriage?

Mellie also did not want to risk being called a prostitute. It was assumed that any woman walking out of a marriage was solely to engage in promiscuity. A divorcee was taken to be difficult and unmarriageable. Such a woman would be treated as an outcast. She would be blamed, even if her husband had been at fault. A woman such as this was not allowed to continue partaking of all the sacraments as expected of all good Catholics. Mellie was a woman of faith and to be ostracized from her church would be too difficult to handle. Faith was her stronghold.

As time went on Fredrick did find Mellie. Either due to a lack of knowledge of his behavior or a deep-seated understanding that a husband and wife should stay together. He was eventually told by those who knew where his wife was. He never stayed for more than a short time and soon left to look for work and food. But he did come back occasionally and only for moments. And when he did, when he was in any way sorry and apologetic, Mellie received him with open arms. Today was such a day and is on this day that she conceived her last born. Her name was to be Baby.

Reflections: Time for celebration

Take a moment to celebrate your role in your child's life as a father or a mother

To appreciate every life, you have carried in your womb.

Those that cannot celebrate, what is the story?

END OF PART I

~CHAPTER SEVEN~
LIFE BEFORE BABY

Sometimes life feels like a walk through the dusky door of abandonment into the darkness of its loneliness.

As a young mother or dad when job opportunities come your way and you have to leave your child, what do you do to keep connecting with them so that the bond between you and your baby is not affected?

Have you noticed how your child relates to you after you have been away?

Some wounds may last a lifetime and yet healing is possible.
When you feel alone or like others have left you, how do you work through it?

My life has been free. I am a free spirit. I enjoy this state very much. I am hovering and looking at my mother-to-be. I do not know what is attracting me to this family. I think I would like to be born here. Every child is unique and so I will be. This couple has had four boys previously and I am wondering if I want to be a boy like the others before me or not. I fear my father to be. His anger and violence always reach me somehow. I feel it is going to be confining in this human body. Life can be different because of my uniqueness. I have a role to play. I am on a mission to make a difference in that family and the world by being, though I am not sure how. Actually, I am reluctant to let it happen. It is like I am pushed by a force beyond me.

In a moment of peace, of stillness within the storm of Fredrick's drunken violence, Mellie welcomes Fredrick back into her life. And it was on that night that Mellie again became pregnant. This was the ninth and final pregnancy for Mellie.

It has happened. I am fused, with both energies. I am resting in my mother's womb. I am finally here. Even though I have had some warm and nice times, too often I have a feeling of dread to be confined, feeling helpless, needing protection and feeling unsafe. I feel very tense at times and very exposed to death and harm. Today I had a dreadful experience. My dad is running after us. He wants to rip open my mum's womb and kill me. I am very scared. My mum is scared too.

Even though she was heavy with child when the chasing began, Mellie ran like a cheetah. Every time Fredrick drank, he chased. However, for even with a child she was too fast for a drunkard like him.

This night, she made for her brother's wife Naomi's house about two kilometers away. This sister-in-law was also used to these kinds of episodes from her husband, known as 'those days'. It is believed by many that men who love their wives at times needed to prove how strong they were by battering them. When Mellie arrived, her protector immediately understood the situation and she was taken in. Fredrick had his usual machete. Mellie was pushed by her protector into the bedroom and under the bed. Before long Fredrick arrived, kicking down the door cursing and swearing. As he stood in the doorway, with only Mellie's protector and the feeble hiding place of the bed between him and her. Fredrick swore he would surely kill her if he found her in this house. The words came whining from his lips, "I swear by God I will rip your fetus from your womb if I find you here. Get out quick. I am warning you, get out and come back to me. Do you see this shiny sword? I know you are under this bed. Mellie! Get out now!" Mellie did not want to test what he was capable of.

He turned to face the direction of the house owner. "I will kill you too for aiding her as I saw her run towards this direction. Tell me where she is hiding now or else."

But the sister-in-law stood her ground, assuring Fredrick that Mellie was not in the house. He ignored her and pushed past her. He was now in the house, searching. He walked straight to the bedroom. The room was dark. Sword in hand, he kneeled down to reach under the bed. Using the sword, he slashed from side to side, reaching as far underneath the bed as he could, feeling for her, feeling for the connection between blade and her flesh. Mellie squeezed into one corner of the bed as tight as she could. She pushed against the wall. She could hardly breathe. Her heart was pounding as she prayed that the sword would not touch her or her baby. She sucked in her stomach as much as she could to protect the baby. She was so heavily pregnant! With a month plus to go.

My mother is expectant with me. I feel like I am being pushed out. I cannot go out now, no! ... Not now. I am not ready to go out. It is too dangerous out there. My mother is getting tense and is trying to pull her tummy in. As she holds her breath, her heart is pumping and so is mine. I am tense too; I feel the squeeze. My time, it seems, has come.

Fredrick continued to slash until his arm became tired. He then rose angrily and slashed around aimlessly, infuriated by his failed attempt. Was he going to pull the bed? What else could he do? Mellie with the help of her hands pushed her tummy in. She turned towards the wall to hide her abdomen – her baby.

I now know that I have to save my mother so I hang on, curl myself into a tight ball and be more determined to stay in. I know that if my mother lives so will I.

Mellie waited and listened keenly. She had not realized he had stumbled outside of the house and disappeared. *Oh! We are still here! We have not died.* After what seemed forever Naomi called from the door, 'Mellie, come out. Your lover has left!' this was their way of speaking to ease the tension. 'Fredrick thinks he is wiser than us, look at us now.' Naomi said as she winked at her 'partner in crime' imitating him and twisting her waist. They laughed but Mellie cautioned Naomi as she still felt he could change his mind and turn back. Women had a way of coping in the midst of all this day to day disturbances.

I have always been scared of death. I always fear for my mother. If she dies, I will die too. Many a time I feel it close. I fear and I am sensitive to even the slightest noise. Noise is always an indication of danger. I always know when my father comes home. When he is around, I just freeze. I am frozen with fear and I do not stir. I have learned to hide by pretending I do not exist. I am the quiet child who does not fuss over anything on the outside. What they do not know is that inside, inside I am dying already.

I have always known dad's voice well even before I saw him. I know the unique sound of the stumping of his feet, his whistling and whining tone of voice. I can even sense him looking at us angrily. I do not know why he is always angry with mom. I feel like his piercing eyes can see me even in here. I do not feel safe whenever I am in his presence. Father is loud when he drinks, which now is nearly always. If he is not drinking he does not talk and so I do not hear him. The only voice I know of him is his angry voice.

How I wish at times that the earth could open up and swallow me. I consider going back. I feel small and helpless whenever my father looks at me. I do not know who I am in his presence. All I see are dad's condemning eyes. I feel humiliated and ashamed of whom I am. I tremble as cold engulfs me like a chicken in the rain. I squeeze in all the more to disappear further into the womb!

His eyes watch me.

They are not big eyes
They are small and ugly

They say more than words
They look and I freeze
Then I look back in disgust

Why can't I use words?
I am afraid, I can't speak
The eyes take my voice away
Their look makes me angry
They look and I get mad

They look and I remain silent.
Those eyes say, say words
Mine say silently, 'I hate you'
'What are you staring at?'
'Do not look at me like that'

'I am scared, I don't feel safe.'
I feel threatened to the core
I feel they can see through me
I feel nailed to the spot
My legs are like lead

I cannot run
I am too afraid of the outside
And yet can I face those eyes
I have nothing to say
It is not bravery but cowardice.

Both my mother and I have come to the verge of death. I cannot afford to lose her. I know, for me to live I need to mind her. It is my duty to protect us! I do not believe at times even God has as much responsibility as I have for mom!!!

A few weeks after that episode, her labor began. The pain lasted the whole night. The labor pains began in the early hours of the day and it wasn't until nearly the next morning at dawn that Baby eventually appeared. It was clear she was fighting back.

The time has eventually come for me to be born; I do not want to face this world. I am unwilling to go. I will not go. But I have to go to help reduce her pain and mine. I may as w...e...l...l pop o...u...t!

I am very cold. I shake and shake with cold and I get warm with Mother's breast. I will not cause any trouble. I better remain as quiet as a mouse. I do not cry and mom thinks I am such a calm child. The truth is I am scared. I do not want to attract unnecessary attention.

When Baby finally arrived, her father was not around and so could not name her as was the custom. Consequently, Fredrick did not turn up for a few days. On the second day, Mellie had the baby baptized. She took on the task of choosing her baby a name after her daughter who had died as a baby some years before. Her name was to be Baby.

What was similar between her sister and her, she does not know. Is that why she found it difficult to come into this world? Because she was a reincarnation of her already deceased sister? Maybe she did not want to come and be taken as her dead sister. Did her mother see her as her other daughter reincarnated or was she here in her own right and capacity?

Imagine! They have named me after my sister. But my sister is dead. Do they know what this has done to me? I am scared of death. I knew it before my time. It is like death is so part of me and it scares me. How connected am I with my namesake sister? So, my parents see me not for me but as the child that never was. I feel too much is expected of me as a child and I am already tired of being expected to be my sister. I am Baby!!!

Perhaps it was the feeling that she was not her own self, perhaps it was the intense fear she experienced in the womb. Whatever it was, Baby was born with an innate kind of fear that she carried with her wherever she went.

She feared everything she did not know and much of what she did know. When Baby was able to walk long enough to go and visit her mother at work, she would go with her brother Mato. A giant bridge two lanes wide inclusive of spacious pedestrian paths on either side crossed a great river. During the rainy season, the river would roar and run brown with mud picked up by the overflow. During the dry season it would run silent, underground, showing no signs on the surface.

The first time Baby saw the bridge was just after the rainy time of year when the river ran fiercely. She froze when she saw it, looming overhead. There was a concrete mystery on an otherwise earthen road. It was the only smooth, concrete ride for a car within 50 kilometers.

"What is the matter, with you Baby?" he asked her.

"I will drop! Hold me!" As she said this, a car moved past them. She closed her eyes and held Mato so tight that he could not move. "Hold me! The bridge will collapse!" she cried out.

"Now surely Baby, you are a small thing and see that car is huge, how can you make this strong bridge to collapse?" But she held firm, "I know it will fall from under us." They spent close to an hour there the first day, Mato trying to convince Baby and Baby refusing. Finally, Mato threatened to never take her again to see their mother if she did not cross. It was the only way to persuade her to cross the bridge, and it was a threat often repeated.

It took her a long time to get used to crossing that bridge and many journeys were slowed greatly when they came upon that place. But

Mato was patient with her and whenever they got there he knew she would need to hold him and cross slowly. She feared when she had to do something in front of people. She froze in the presence of others. She had such low self-esteem; she apologized for her every act. She was so self-conscious that it could at times paralyze her.

Once, she was asked to read at the school assembly. For the whole day before her reading, she could not settle. She was planning how she would stand, how she would speak, how she would breathe. How could she read in the presence of hundreds of people? How, she did not know, but she managed to read after a few moments of silence in front of everyone. Afterwards, she felt so ashamed. She judged her every action and scrutinized her every decision. She did not read in the school assembly ever again.

Whatever it is really
Some call it fear.
Or when nerves won't work freely
I'll call it fear my dear

Weakness as soon as you are up
Fear tells you everyone is all eyes
And at the thought of it, your eyes droop
The heart beats faster, as skin emits a thin sweat of ice

The eyes see double
The crowd seems to multiply
One feels single and all others in a couple
And the heat will surely reply

Know seven days earlier you'll read
And for several days, in your stomach, butterflies will fly
When it finally comes, the knees dance

The mouth runs dry and the tongue won't comply

You may not know what I mean
This's the shoe I've always worn
Where it pinches I know, it's not a dream
Now it no longer fits and should be thrown.

This final pregnancy was complicated for Mellie. Juggling work, children and Fredrick led to her losing her job in the final months of the pregnancy. Mellie didn't learn till later that she actually wasn't fired for this, but because another worker was jealous of her and told lies about her. Initially, they were believable but after investigation, it was discovered they were untrue. By then, another lady had Mellie's job.

The other lady that replaced her didn't last the year and afterwards, her employer returned to Mellie and asked if she could come back to work.

Her pride said no but her need said yes. She would have to work harder; she would have to ensure her children ran the house themselves when she wasn't there. It was to be a difficult set of years but nothing could compare to the years before.

By now Baby was ten months old. Mellie had loved taking care of her child but she couldn't afford to stay with Baby at home because she would lose her job. But how could she leave her baby? She must choose the job. Baby, who was too young yet to live with her siblings, had to move in with Mellie's godmother.

The choice for Mellie was between her baby and her new job. She was between a rock and hard place but a choice had to be made. Staying with her Baby meant no job while the job ensured food on the table for her whole family.

I feel sad to be away from you, my mother. I need you to hold me, my mother. When I cry there is no one here to see and comfort me.

I feel alone and lost. Mother, I do not know anyone here. I do not know this place. I need to feel your warmth as you hold me. I feel shaken and hurt. I am angry at you, my mother. Why have you preferred work to me? Do I not matter to you? I want to be with you... do not leave me alone. Naku (please)... do not go and leave me... what have I done to deserve this pain. Mother...please, do not go... I will miss you!

No matter what I do, you will still go! Fine then... go. Baby's mood went back and forth. She loved and needed her mother, but she hated her for leaving. *Fine then... go,* she would think and feel. Whenever she did, her lower lip swelled and began to shake. Her eyes welled up... one drop ... then another, then a stream of tears. *I want to cry, but is there any point? Crying will not bring you back.* Baby learned to swallow her pain and stop her tears! For the next few hours after each time Mellie left, Baby would watch the gate. Eventually, giving up and turning away. Her mother would never come back for her.

But Mellie had to go! She was employed. Duty was duty and it had to be attended to. Every day Mellie had to choose between her employer and her toddler. There was a job to be done for the employer and there was a toddler to raise.

Her breasts hurt as she was still breastfeeding. Mellie spent sleepless nights thinking and missing her baby. She found it difficult to concentrate without wondering how her baby was. It hurt so much. She had disturbing dreams. When she woke up her eyes were tired and her body too heavy to move around from chore to chore. She had to force her mind to stay present to what she was doing each time as her heart was at home with her baby.

It is always lonely being home without mom. I miss her. I do not see any other children. I do not know who I am or to whom I belong. Neither do I even know who my mother is. Do I even have a mother? I miss being cared for, cleaned. I miss being cuddled and tucked into bed at night. No one changes my wet and dirty clothes and I at times cry myself to sleep. I do most of this by myself. There are lots of animals around.

Mother, I do not know anyone here. All the people here are strangers. I am just left to sit here and they go away. Subsequently, I do not trust them. They leave me all the time. I do not see my siblings. I keep to myself. I have discovered a world of my own. I spend a lot of my time alone. I have made friends with some insects and some other animals with me. I especially like the birds. They are free, flying up in the sky. I wish I were a bird. I really like being on my own. I imagine a friend and talk to them when playing. I know lots of insects, worms, birds and some animals. I have learned to cope through being creative. I mold. I miss you, my mother, terribly.

Sometimes I do not know where my mother is or whether Mwaitu is alive or dead. I do not believe she will come back. She has not been here to see me take my first step or even to hear the first word I uttered. I often wonder what my first word was as I had no 'Mwaitu' (mom) to call."

Mellie worked at a school some way away. Initially, she came home occasionally for nights and mostly for weekends. The school year was increasingly busy as it neared its end and Mellie needed to be gone for some time. She didn't know when she would return.

Mellie worked tirelessly. She worked during the holidays. She needed to make ends meet. She ground the maize for the students, she cooked and because the water was a problem she boiled it and gave water to all the students. She took the ill to the hospital daily and was on call at night as a matron. Work was hard but truth be told she enjoyed the financial freedom that came after the hard work. It brought her a value she hadn't felt in a long time. But for the pain of leaving behind her youngest child, she loved her work.

Finally, after the school closed for the long holidays and everything was sorted out, Mellie returned to Baby. But when she appeared Baby walked away. Baby no longer knew her own mother.

Panicked, Mellie followed her baby, calling for her. "Baby! Baby! It is I, your mom, your Mellie. Remember me? Come, it is your mom. Come, my Baby, mom is here". Baby just toddled away, crying bitterly. When Mellie reached her, she picked her up and held her against her chest. "Come, my Baby. It is me, your mother."

Who is this strange woman coming towards me? I feel scared. I do not go to strangers. Go away and leave me alone. Why are you coming to me? I do not want anyone near me. Who are you, woman? Why are you being so nice to me?

Mellie held Baby's little heart against her own, helping to rest the child's small head on her neck. Mellie rubbed her back in a circular motion as both cried for what seemed ages. Eventually Baby began to calm down and Mellie tried offering Baby her breast. But Baby only placed her lips on the nipple. She didn't open her mouth to suck. Baby sniffed her mother. She seemed to remember the smell.

As she alternated between sobbing and calmly sniffling, Mellie sang *"Kalumaita kakwa i lulu kilya, kana kilyai lulu, mwaitu nuyu i lulu kilya kana i lulu lului lulu!" (My little last born, lulu calm down. Calm down my baby lulu! For mother is here lulu lului lulu!).*

Mellie had brought Baby a flowery dress and some yellow scones. It was a nice treat for Baby and that afternoon both spent as much time as they could together. After Baby was put to bed and Mellie was back in the main room she broke down. Mellie cried so much she was inconsolable.

How could her own child turn away from her? She actually turned away and followed the calves. Baby did not know her own mother. Mellie began to count in her mind how many months she had been away from her child. Her tears tasted as bitter as bile. She could not believe her own child did not recognize her! She kept an eye on her to reassure her.

With Fredrick gone for years Mellie placed Baby on her bed. She too had missed her daughter so much. Baby stirred every few minutes to feel for her mother's body. If she did not feel her, she sat up and without a sound, tears begun to fall down her little cheeks. Her mother noticed, picked her in her arms and calmed her down.

But I do know her. Or at least I knew her once. I do not trust her. I do not trust her and I am afraid to reconnect with her in case I lose her again. But she's so nice, the warmth, the care. I think she really cares, but I know it will not last. If I keep safe and protected against this hurt I will survive. I cannot feel that hurt again.

It took several weeks before Baby could warm up to this woman who was her mother. Mellie promised herself never to be away from her child for that long ever again. From now on she would come home every weekend if she could, or at least every other weekend.

Reflection Time: Abandonment

While Mellie's new job is a blessing for the family it also becomes a life's journey. That interval between her mother leaving and her eventual returning seemed so long for Baby- it felt to her like.... death.

A connection is on the other side of abandonment. This is a difficulty when one feels alone. Having some close connection with someone like a counsellor who can hold the space while engaging with this difficulty of feeling left alone helps us stabilize.

Abandonment at a young age is deeply rooted and is ingrained in the flesh or body. Everyone's journey is unique and one needs to do their own releasing in order to make different conscious choices today especially in relation to reaching out.

Whom can you reach out to? Reach out to someone who will respect you and hear what you feel.

Remember that:

You did not do anything to make them leave you.

You are special.

When you were left, you were only a child and could not do much for yourself.

You the grown up can get support for yourself now.

Someone out there is waiting for your call.

Now you can stay; do not leave yourself like they did.

~CHAPTER EIGHT~
LONELINESS

What story surrounds your birth?

I invite you to find out as much as you can about your earliest separation from your primary caregiver especially the females … (This may help you understand yourself deeper in the way you react and how you do things today).

I would like to be with this woman I am told to call mum. I feel pulled to her and I never want to let her go. But I somehow think she will not stay. She is bound to leave again, just like she did before. I will be disappointed again. She always leaves me! She keeps going and for so long then comes back. Why can she not take me with her?

It took some time but Baby did eventually allow her mom to come near her. When she did, it was as if a barrier was broken. She felt good but she would not trust her heart. Something was lost between them and she was sad. They wept and wept. They both felt so lost. Baby was learning hard lessons.

We are together but still, I cannot allow her completely into my heart. I feel cold and distant. I feel confused and do not need you anymore. I would like to connect with you but I do not know what to do. I am angry at you. You keep coming close and before too long you disappear again. My heart hurts and is too cold to feel. I am stuck. I am too hurt to talk. You do not notice I am hurt. Am I the reason you leave me? How do I keep minding myself when I am so small? I missed you very much. I find it hard to let you know how sad I feel to have lost in my heart a place for you. My stomach feels sunken. My arms refuse to reach out to you in case I need you. They are too heavy to lift. I cannot tell you how much I need you, even though I cannot trust you. I need your touch. I don't need your touch. I feel sad to have lost this and I am scared to need you, mother. I do not know how to move on from here.

Baby wasn't sure this was going to last. It felt too good to be trusted. She learned to enjoy her mother's company when she had it but didn't expect it to last. This part was always complicated for both. As the holidays grew on she began to bond with her mother more but when the school opened again and Mellie was called away those fragile bonds shattered. It was not a feeling of betrayal mixed with anger but also a feeling of loss and loneliness. Baby longed for her mother more than anything else in her life. In all this Baby still felt she couldn't show her mother that she needed her. Mellie was always going to go away again. There was no point. Baby couldn't bear looking into her mother's eyes anymore lest Mellie saw the sadness they hid. When Mellie did leave for school at the beginning of the school year Baby shut down and decided she had to mind herself; she locked her soul and kept the key. She decided to only let in people on her own terms.

So, she coiled inwards and within this inwardness, she felt safe.

Just before Mellie left, she took Baby to their real house, their home on Mellie's stepbrother's land. Here Baby met her siblings; Mulili, Loki, Ally and Mato. The new house scared Baby for there were no neighbors. No other people around and all that surrounded them was the jungle.

My brother narrates very interesting stories even though they give me nightmares. He always tells me these stories at night. Although they scare me witless when I go to bed, I cannot stop listening to them.

I only have to do one chore and that is to bring firewood into the kitchen. I usually play during the day and before I know it, it is already dark. I like sitting by the fire. The firewood is just beside the kitchen door, about three steps away. They go 'Baby, go for the firewood.' I always dread these words! They say them dutifully every single night!

I have always been told stories about the hyena. This is an animal I have never seen but still, Dear God, I fear it like death. As soon as I step outside the door, they always say 'Baby! Mr. Hyena!'

As soon as I hear those words, I reverse into the door like a shot and with only one or two sticks in my hand. I never turn outside the door. I shoot in the same way I had gone out to ensure I guard myself against the 'hyena'. I plead with them and even promise a sweet when mom comes so that they will take me out but everyone has their own duties. I find my chore the most difficult. I usually promise to carry in all the firewood 'tomorrow' from very early in the morning. However, the days seem shorter and I attend to matters of greater importance to me – play till evening comes. These evenings come too soon! Then when night comes, my heart is in my mouth. Many a time, this is my nightly cross!

As Baby and her siblings grew up they learned how to pray. Whenever their mother was at home, they said their night prayers. They took turns leading except for Baby. Mellie would normally politely intercept if she wanted to pray for a special intention. They sometimes woke up earlier than usual to say the morning prayers. They liked saying the rosary together. Their mother always had the rosary in her hands, rolling the beads between her fingers as she walked. One day, as Baby and her mother walked through the paths in the jungle, Baby got interested in the ever-moving rosary beads in her mother's hand and asked her mother how she knew which mysteries of the rosary to pray. Mellie just smiled and told her it was a case of remembering, of memorizing each one. Baby decided she would look up the mysteries of the rosary in a prayer book and try to memorize them. She could not make out how her mother could remember all the many mysteries.

Prayer was part and parcel of what they did. It took time but all Mellie's children learned to appreciate the discipline of prayer. Prayer before chores and grace before and after meals. Evening prayers before bed.

During these years, as life settled into the routine that would come to be normal, as Mellie's job took her to and from the house at a regular – and now more frequent – basis, Baby got used to living in the jungle. She discovered that she did have neighbors. The distance from one home to the other was great, the nearest being Mellie's stepbrother's house. But they were still neighbors.

Baby grew attuned to the sounds of birds and wild animals. She began to learn what each sound belonged to and from where it originated. Even so, though they were familiar Baby was still afraid of nearly everything in the jungle – big and small. The thick wall of trees and sounds which surrounded them was a threatening force and something Baby feared greatly. Sometimes her brothers left her and went to a nearby town to the cinema. It seemed to have been a boys' only cinema as Baby was never allowed to go – she was young but most of all she was a girl. All she knew of it was what her brothers said the day after. Something about 'Kung Fu' and 'Bruce Lee'. Baby did not know what these words meant. They would go before dusk. And, when the setting sun cloaked the jungle in darkness and revealed only its sounds, Baby would be left at home.

I am in the house. I am too afraid to even light the lantern. I am afraid someone may peep in and see me on my own. I do not know how to cook so since my brother has not cooked, I will sleep hungry tonight. Whenever there is a cinema in the nearby town, which is monthly I sleep alone and hungry.

My heart drops whenever I hear them talk about the next time they go to the cinema. This is because I will be left alone again. It is very scary to be alone. I listen to all the sounds of animals and all the other sounds. The only domestic animals we have here are the chickens. I wish we did not have them sometimes.

Tonight, this predator is here to prey on the chickens. The chicken house is near our house. I can hear the chickens making this deafening noise. Can you hear that? I have just remembered there is no one else in the homestead but me. I freeze with fear. I do not know what to do. It seems like it is going to feed on all the chickens. With every increasing noise, I wrap myself tighter with my blanket. I think this animal will come and attack me next. Although I have locked the door tightly and pushed several seats to make sure nothing can come in, I am still scared. I guard myself until I slowly fall asleep.

I wake up in the morning when the sun is high. By now my brothers are up. Five big hens have been killed. I tell them how scared I felt last night when I heard the chickens being eaten up! My brothers start making fun of me about the way I shouted last night. I did not know I shouted. I wish they were there with me. I miss them here at night especially. I do not feel safe at all. I am not happy I was born at this time. I wish I had a small brother or sister. Every other week this animal comes back and the same happens. Sometimes I feel like screaming but I think maybe the animal will find me so I just swallow my fear. My brothers are too big for me to question. When they come they make fun of my fear and I get angry. They do not hear what I say - that I fear being on my own. There is no point of telling them anyway as they will still go when they need to go. I feel trapped here. I wish they did not leave me. So, I feel scared over and over again. I don't know what to do!

You know, I like daylight and wish all nights were days because as soon as the sun sets, my fear sets in. Sometimes I wonder why they are not afraid of the nights like I am and wish they were. If they were, they would have to remain with me. At least there would be more of us scared when fear came. During the day I am usually home alone. I do not know where my siblings are a lot of times. I think when you are big you do not bother telling your young sister where you go! There is this tree about four meters from my house. When there is no one here, I climb up on it. I have a pillow and a sheet on a coiled branch which I use to sit but mostly lie on. This is where I sleep most of the time during the day.

When any visitor comes, I pretend there is nobody at home. They say "Hodi," meaning 'may I come in'. I do not answer unless it is a family member. Whenever my family is around I make a swing from the branch of this tree and play there until I feel dizzy. I love this tree very much. It is strong, always green and always there for me. From this tree of mine, I can see far out into the jungle and I dream of my future."

Around the time Baby turned eight, her brothers gave her the nickname 'Ngoto' because she was skinny and had long legs. This is a name given to a bird that they said looked like her. It was a tall skinny bird with even longer and skinnier legs. The bird would come to the house several times during the week and land on a nearby tree. Then it would start singing its melodious song. Baby, who grew up mimicking the bird calls and animal noises as a way to stave off the fear of the jungle, loved this melodious song and at times would sing along with her own lyrics. She felt protection for this bird and a personal bond. When her brothers called her by its name or sang the song it would trigger her anger. *Ngoto syaendie maasiisii masiii masiisiisisi 'Ngoto went to Masiisii masiii masiisiisisi'*. It was sung to the tune that Ngoto played and it would anger Baby because it was her song and it saddened her that the bird would soon leave.

When it first began, she really would get mad at them for singing it. Even whistling the melody would get her going. To get her own back, she would call them nicknames which she knew they did not like. The most annoying brother she called, 'Kyongo', meaning 'big head' and since the other did not annoy her as much, she rarely called him 'Kilomo', meaning 'big lips'.

Mellie had a nickname for Baby that she truly loved. It was 'ilumaita yakwa', meaning 'my last born'. It made her feel very special and loved. She would sit on her mother's lap while her mother stroked her hair; even at the age of eight when she had grown so tall that her legs would touch the ground. Her brothers would make fun of her for this but she just rested on her mother's breast and made faces at her brothers, sometimes mouthing the words 'Kyongo' and 'Kilomo'.

When they weren't secretly fighting they would sit together and Ally would tell stories. Storytelling was a strong part of Kamba culture and often teachings could be found within the stories. Baby would do anything to listen to Ally's stories of the animals, including sharing her scones or sweets.

She particularly liked the story about the hare and the hyena. In most stories, the hare was depicted as wise while the hyena was foolish and did not think through issues. The story went like this:

Once upon a time, there lived two friends, the hare and the hyena. They used to share everything, including food. Times became very hard and it was becoming more and more difficult to find food, for a great famine had reached the land. The hare met the hyena and said 'Mr. Hyena, as you have noticed it is really difficult these days to find food. Many days we come home empty-handed having spent the day in the scourging sun. I have one suggestion. We need to kill our mothers so that the little we get will only be for two mouths to feed. What do you think?' The Hyena thought for a while and eventually agreed. He thought if he killed his mother he would have more food for himself!

The Hyena went home and hit his mother to death. The Hare, however, hid his mother and in pretense put rubbish in a bag and started hitting hard. When the Hyena heard the sound, he hit his mother harder to join in with the Hare. When they met the next day, the Hyena was very sad and hardly said a word. He was very grieved. The hare continued feeding his mother until the famine was over and then took her out. The Hyena could not believe his eyes when he saw his friend's mother. He cried and cried until his eyes were as red as beetroot.

Though explanations were rarely given, everyone listening knew this is about the need to critique what others advise us to do, to not simply do it, even if that means jeopardizing the relationships we have with some of our friends. We can say no, wisely.

But for Baby, this was not of importance and the story was not a metaphor. She would listen to this story and cry. She could not imagine how someone could think of killing their own mother. She would think of her mother and sob even harder. For the aim of African folklore was also to evoke importantly desired human values in this particular story; love, care, altruism and more. The story would also repel a child from communally undesirable vices like selfishness, meanness and such like.

Despite this, she could not stop listening to the stories. "Please Ally, tell me again," she would say amid tears. And he never disappointed. When Ally was in a good mood, which was most of the time, he always had a story for them all. Some were so sad they cried; others were so funny they laughed until their ribs ached; some were so scary that Baby was afraid to go to bed.

One of the advantages of being the last born was that one went to sleep before the rest of the family. Baby would be able to fall asleep in her bed with the muffled sound of adults talking outside the room. Though she was scared, as long as they were there she felt somewhat safe.

Her mother continued to come home whenever she could and when Mellie was home, Baby would lie near the open fire and pretend to be very drowsy. Her mother would then turn to Baby's brothers and command them, "Prepare the food fast, the baby needs to sleep."

Ally would then start calling her by her nickname or whistling to her in the song he knew she didn't like. "Ngoto. A child? Your work is only to eat," then he would whistle softly.

"How many times have I cautioned you against whistling at night?" Their mother would shout from the main house. "Ally, why is the child crying?" Mellie would ask when she was in the room. Ally would simply shrug his shoulders. For a long time, Mellie did not know what made Baby cry whenever Ally sang or whistled the song of the Ngoto bird.

When Baby was nearer to her mother she would make faces at Ally but at other times, like tonight, it was too big of a risk. All it took was Mellie to turn away for the fighting to start.

Usually, Baby was ok. She was always delighted that Ally would have to cook fast for her whenever Mellie told him. It made up for all the times he called her 'Ngoto'.

Reflection Time: Separation at an early age

Separation at an earlier age affects a child. This is a reality for Baby in this chapter. It does not matter whether it is for a genuine reason as in the case of Mellie (job) or not. To the child, it means a disconnection from the source of love. This could affect a child's ability to trust.

You may notice your child does not want to be with you anymore'

How do you want to engage with your child to mend your relationship?

What about you the grown-up reader who feels resentment for your parent because you feel they gave you away and did not give you care or love when you needed them?

What "if anything" do you want to heal while your parent is still alive?

And if your parent has gone what do you need to forgive them for?

CHAPTER NINE~ STARTING SCHOOL

What do you need to do to be able to appreciate your parents?
What was not so relationally helpful that you may need healing in, to make the home a safe place for you?

Pretty soon Mellie had earned enough and Baby was grown up enough to go to school. Until now she had been left at home while her two siblings were at school and she was excited to join them. She got all dressed up and carried a big bag. It was the feeling and the excitement of school.

My first day to go to school has come. Somehow I have forgotten about mom for some time now. I have been lonely at home as I am always left alone until the evening when my siblings come back from school. Oh! I cannot wait to go 'to the big school'. I cannot wait to carry a very big school bag like my brothers. I think that this is the greatest achievement. I am carrying my school bag which has some food for me to eat later. I am in a new school uniform. I feel really good, I am just running after the other children. I have not been on this part of the road before. I am near a big school.

The bell is ringing. The bigger children are running past me like mad people. They are saying that everyone has to obey the bell and so they are running. If anyone does not obey the bell, they face consequences and are beaten senselessly. So, they run off. I follow at a slower pace. As I run, I see this object in front of me.

It is huge; it walks on its fours towards me. I have never in my life seen this. I am scared and so I am grounded. I watch as I am dumbfounded.

The other pupils are passing by like it is very normal as they run off to school. This thing has stopped too. I yell "Let me pass!" To my amazement, it is speaking back to me. I can hear in-between yells, "little child pass." Did he just talk? That scares me more. I yell louder to the top of my voice. I do not know that this is a man. I think it is the hyena my brothers always talk to me about. I am very afraid. I did not know Hyenas also talk.

I cry again, "Let me pass please! Let me pass!" The creature is climbing up the side of the road. I still think and feel as though as I pass it might jump at me and kill or eat me up. I am taking careful steps back and forth with my crying eyes transfixed on him. I still cannot get myself to move. If he makes any move, I will scream.

He is now moving into the forest. I cannot see him now. I am moving to the other end of the road as far away as I can. I pass as a warplane, screaming loudly and running fast.

Baby later learned that the creature she had seen was a man. He had injured his spine while working as a mason and with time he had become disabled and had to walk on his hands and feet. That morning, he was going from one of his wives' home to the other's home.

Where Mellie and her children lived there were two wet seasons which opened the flood gates of heaven and poured down the rain onto their little house. Since their roof was grass-thatched and not of iron, the grass needed to be replaced as least once a year. To do this, Mellie needed to cut grass from the school compound during her off days. This grass was then transported by a tractor to her home.

She did this dutifully each time it was needed. One day a teacher working in the same compound enquires from her, "Mellie, do you never stop cutting grass? Why do you not have an iron roof?"

Mellie did not hesitate to say, "Do not worry; only God knows! You know only a stone stays put."

Mellie, unlike other women in her village, was a salaried woman. Her salary meant that she had enough money to educate her children, but not much else. It was either education or luxuries like iron roofs; luxuries which made the house colder. Educating children in her village, especially educating girls, was seen as a strange endeavor and Mellie was the only woman keen enough to educate her children. Because of this, the villagers kept asking why, given that there are no jobs. "Why do you educate your children instead of buying a piece of land? They are not any different from us. We hang out with them sure even though we have no education ourselves."

After all, they thought, Mellie was not even on her own land.

But Mellie did what she felt was right and what she felt was right was the education of her children.

Meanwhile, Fredrick had fallen into the backs of their minds. He was elsewhere, picking coffee to earn a living in the coffee-growing province. He only had to mind one mouth and it was much easier and more manageable than the headache of feeding many children, dressing them and educating them.

This all changed right around the time Baby started school. He decided to visit for the first time since Baby's birth.

At this time, there were only three kids at home. Mulili and Loki had moved on, seeking better lives near the coast. When he turned up, only Baby and her next brother were home. He introduced himself to them as their dad. They did not know what to say to him so they gave him a chair to sit in as they waited under a tree for further instructions from Ally, the oldest and wisest of the brothers at home. Mato and Baby had grown to accept that they only had a mother. Dad was a new concept.

Ally didn't come home till the evening, by which point Mellie had already arrived and greeted her long-lost husband. Ally went to Mellie and whispered "Mum, who is that old 'Mzee?"

She replied, "That is your 'au' (dad)."

Accordingly, Baby and Mato started calling him "Ally's au", not knowing that he was theirs as well.

Mellie had never mentioned him; why would she? Baby had thought every other child like her had only one parent. They, therefore, weren't expecting him nor missing him. To endear himself to them he decided to take Mato and Baby out the following day. Ally could not go and was a little more cautious towards this stranger than the other two.

He told them that he works far away in some distant place. He took them on a bus, the first bus they had ever used.

What is this bus that can move so fast? These trees are flying past us all. I am so scared but I am also fascinated by the world around me. When they arrived near where he worked, he gave them some money to spend on food and soda. *What is the drink I am consuming? It is so strange and fizzy.*

This was a different day for the children and when they got back they talked of the wonders they saw until their eyelids fell over their eyes. They were very tired of visiting new places. Fredrick stayed on for a few days and then left. Baby remembered he was dressed in a black, striped suit. He was going back to wherever he came from. Just like mother and just like everybody else; he left too!

The children did not see him again until Baby was about thirteen. It was as if the prodigal son was returning, except he was the husband and he was not in any way remorseful. Life was very comfortable and peaceful before the return of Fredrick. Then one afternoon, Baby arrived home from school to find that he had returned. She couldn't really remember him well but she remembered a bus journey to faraway towns. It didn't matter to Baby anyway. Everybody eventually left and he would be gone soon too.

Except for this time, he didn't. Days became weeks and weeks became months. He did not leave.

From the start, he made sure that all the family knew who was in charge. He made hard and fast rules. Before long, he was comfortable enough to start drinking. He didn't care that his brother had forbidden him to live on the land. With drinking came the spending of money. He had to know where everyone was going and demanded to know what was being spent, to budget every single cent his wife earned.

Baby waited and waited for him to go back. She, along with everyone else, waited in hope that he would do as he had done before. But this time it did not happen. Everyone's patience was wearing thin! What Baby didn't know was that her brother Ally had gone looking for their father from the coffee province. He was approaching his twenties and felt that he needed his dad to show him how to be a man. Without informing anyone, he had travelled far to look for him, found him and pleaded with him to come back home.

Oh! My freedom is gone since this man came. I fear him and I feel hindered from being myself. I feel trapped. I cannot breathe. He shuts me up and even though I do not talk much now I feel less concerned. We do not have fun anymore. I want to leave the house and stay away from home. Being at home is not enjoyable anymore. Accounting for everything is tiring. I can neither think nor feel anymore.

Baby didn't know what to do. Only she and another brother were in primary school. Before Fredrick, it was difficult for their mom to educate and provide for them, and now it was almost impossible. Their father made everyone feel his presence. He stayed at home and interfered with everyone's business as he saw fit. When it came to going to church, he said people were hypocritical. Gradually, he stopped anyone who wanted to attend religious ceremonies. Baby hated when he drank because his tongue was loosened and he became shameless. She often wished she could close her ears.

One time his son told him, "Please if you ever need to say anything to me, say it when you are sober, dad."

They really believed that he said a lot of stuff when drunk because he lacked the courage to say it when sober. Whenever he oiled himself, he would direct his disappointment at their mother. "Mellie I can see that your sons have become men enough to challenge me."

Fredrick was used to doing the talking while his family listened and not the other way around. When this did not work, he would swear and curse and hit Mellie.

Nau (my father) says that women have no brains and so my mother does not have any brains as she is only a woman. This is so annoying. I get really angry when I hear this. How dare you say that about my Star? I will prove to you that women have brains. I am determined that I will never be your fool. Daddy, do you know how this hurts to hear you call mother names? Where did you come *from? I am tired of listening to this. I have decided to switch off and just avoid you. Daddy, I need you to hear and respect me*

When you say hurting words about mother you hurt me too as a woman and I feel not respected. Father, listen to me your daughter and let me be. Is it not ok just to be a girl, a daughter? Why do you keep pulling me down?

Seeing Fredrick at home all the time was a constant reminder of feeling unsafe, exposed to hurt, disrespected. She was young and powerless against him. All she could do was be quiet and try to not cause any trouble; anything else had the potential to translate into danger or death or banging of doors.

Hopeless and helpless.

Whenever Fredrick came home, no matter the time or who was in, he demanded fresh food be cooked for him. If nobody answered he could walk to every door and bang until someone responded. If the door wasn't locked – which was rare now – he would pull the individual out and drag them to the chickens, picking one up to be slaughtered for him.

Everyone, especially Baby, made sure their rooms were always locked to ensure Fredrick did not enter unexpectedly to force her to cook at odd hours. Baby had to mind her own boundaries and ensure no uninvited guest crossed her threshold.

Naturally, Baby found it difficult to warm up to her dad. Whenever he laughed at something, she did the opposite. She never wanted him to ever see her teeth. She wore a stone face whenever he was around. She would never talk in his presence. Fredrick had an opinion on everything in this world and the next. He knew – 'knew' – all about religion and always had something religious to say when things didn't go his way. Fredrick would call regular meetings and everyone had to sit in. During these meetings, Baby would switch off. She was just there to be seen in attendance. He did not acknowledge the women in the meeting, nor elsewhere except when to say that they should obey. Baby felt young and helpless. She disagreed silently with him on so many issues but she never knew how to challenge him while also keeping herself safe. She had to strategize very carefully, otherwise, her mother would have to pay for any confrontation or rebellion against his rule. She felt disrespected and made up her mind to keep out of his way, by all means necessary. He became the switch on which she allowed herself to operate.

I'm ashamed of even my mother tongue being spoken. I am ashamed of associating myself with my tribe. I cannot appreciate my mother tongue as most of what I hear spoken is unpalatable. I wish at times I were deaf or do not understand it. I will only speak it only in very close friends' company or when I have no option but to be at home. I do not take pride in my language; it has started to die.

For some time now, Mellie had been saving some money and had recently bought a bull and some goats with the hard-earned cash. One day Fredrick decided to sell the animals they have been keeping because he needed to travel into the country to buy a piece of land. There was no stopping him. Baby didn't even get to say goodbye to the baby goats she had grown to love.

But when Fredrick left it meant that he was gone. That, at least, was a silver lining and they could get back to normal life.

Until two months later when he returned, no title deeds and no money, but drunk as fish. They never dared ask where the money went, or what happened to the land – if there ever was any.

Fredrick believed that men were superior to women and that this was a God-given privilege. According to Fredrick, Mellie knew nothing. He would easily ask his sons for opinions about a certain issue before even thinking of asking Mellie, who was the only earner in the house.

Males were not to help in the kitchen, according to Fredrick. However, by the time he came back home, his sons had already gotten used to doing all the cooking and other housework. To stop this, he sat with his sons and told them stories as Baby struggled to cook and fetch water and collect firewood. He actually punished the boys if they dared sit in the kitchen. They would, he claimed, develop womanly characteristics!

Baby didn't like cooking. It never ended! Hours and hours were spent on cooking something that would be eaten immediately and then the next day the same would happen. A person working in the land was more likely to be appreciated than a person working in the kitchen, even if both worked equally hard. Being in the kitchen meant starting earlier and finishing later than everyone else. When she began, Baby only knew how to make African Tea. Water was mixed with milk and then brought to the boil. Loose tea was added, then lots of sugar. Boil once more, then sieve into a teapot. Next step was to learn Ugali. Arms needed to be strong for Ugali and Baby's arms were not. To prepare it, one had to bring water to boil, adding maize flour little by little while stirring. It was simple in principle but the execution was not. The mixture had to be not too soft but also not too hard. It took a long time to get it right. Sometimes the fire was too high, sometimes it wasn't mixed fast enough. It was like kneading dough, but thicker and with a ladle. Sometimes it was served with meat but mostly it was served with vegetables.

With time, Baby learned to cook, as no one waited on her. Mellie refused to cook as well as work, especially since all the children were big enough and she was exhausted from the day's work. She only cooked on special days like Easter and Christmas. When Fredrick wasn't there, the boys cooked too. In the end, Fredrick began to come and go as before, still staying for longer than he was welcome – which was never – but always leaving at random times for however long he chose.
At least at intermittent times, there was peace.

Reflection Time: Parental Relationships

I have observed that 'hurt people hurt' therefore consciously working through early hurtful situations helps us and those we love. The cycle can be broken.

Can you think of any issues that made you take the first beer or alcohol, or cigarette, bhang or "whatever kind of 'jacket' you wear for protection?"

What were you going through before the first puff or sip?

How do you relate with your children, wife or partner? Children or your loved ones may fear you and not necessarily love you? It is not unusual to feel resentment in helping a parent who was not available for you when you needed him or her. As a grown-up child, how do you change within and heal so that you can be there to provide for parents who only show up when you have made it in life?

~CHAPTER TEN~

SCHOOLING - THE WAY THROUGH

Some children find school stressful and a difficult challenge. The presence of parents provides children with safety they need to negotiate challenges that they meet. The absence too may interfere with a child to be slow or unable to cope.
Each child is different and so they cope with this challenge differently.

What could make a child drop-in performing or out of school?

Do parents listen enough to what could be going on in the life of the child and provide the necessary conditions for the youth to hang in there no matter what they are negotiating in their own life?

The biggest lesson Mellie's children learned over the years was about peace. Their mother could not cope with conflict. She never beat or punished her children. She believed in talking and appealing to her children's best selves in an effort to get them to behave responsibly.

Once, only once did she beat her children. It was a very cold morning and the jungle was just waking up. During this time of their lives, Mato was a truant. He had dropped out of school many times because he didn't bother to show up. Every morning, Baby would organize herself and get ready for school. Mothering everyone dutifully, she would go to the truant's door and call, "Mato, Mato". Sometimes, he would answer and if he did not answer she persisted until he responded. Pretending to be in deep sleep he would grumpily respond an unintelligible response. "Mato, let us go to school" she would plead, at times crying for she knew the importance her mother placed on the school. She cried because she did not like it when her mother was upset. For some reason, she valued education and did not want her brother to miss out. When

Mato got tired of being called he would say, “I feel dizzy”. He was forever dizzy. This was his mantra. Baby knew what he would say but she still kept calling him. After his regular reply, Baby would leave for school with Ally, in tears, feeling very helpless.

That very cold morning, a typical July morning, she woke up as usual. She went as she usually did to call on her brother Mato to go to school. He was dizzy as usual. She went and sat behind their house facing the rising sun, half-waiting for a change she knew wouldn’t come. It felt nice sitting in the warm rays of the sun. The wall of the house was heating up slowly and this spot was well shielded from the cold breeze.

Not long after she sat down – at least it did not feel like long after – Mato came out and for some reason sat beside her. Ally too came and joined them. It was nice. They just sat there and enjoyed the warmth of the rising sun. No one said anything. The animals of the jungle made their customary noises. Baby doodled on the ground and the rest made shapes with whatever was within their reach. Nobody went to school. They all knew they should but somehow the subject was avoided. Ten o’clock came, eleven o’clock came and twelve o’clock came. They had not taken breakfast and by now they just sat, getting weak and drowsy from hunger. There was food to be cooked but they just sat.

It was about noon when they saw their mother appear at the gate. They all ran toward her shouting, “Mwaitu! Mwaitu! Mwaitu!” Mother! Mother! Mother! Why was she back early? This was a lovely surprise. They picked up what she had on her back, shook her and pulled her excitedly from all directions as they walked towards the house.

Mato lit the fire at lightning speed and prepared tea and lunch. In record time, they were all eating like hungry wolves. All this time, Mellie had not talked about school. She had not said anything. The guilty became very uncomfortable. They wished the pregnant silence would be broken. When they had all eaten to their fill, she closed the door and picked up a rope.

What was happening? They squinted as their eyes moved from mother to each other. They had thought since she had not asked them about missing school the issue was gone and forgotten.

She started with Baby and asked her to kneel on a three-legged-stool. Mellie held her rope ready to strike. The other two watched. "Tell me why you did not go to school today," she said.

"They did not go. Thus, I did not" Baby said, half expecting the rope to drop on to her backside. She truly had no reason. This was the first time Baby had missed school. And she had no other reason at all except she had not felt like it. It had been particularly cold this morning – why did she not push herself to leave the house? It was a total miscalculation! Mellie weakly smacked her behind and called on to the next.

Mato had no reason either. Surely, was he, not a perpetual truant? She still did not treat him differently. He got his share. The third, Ally, then stepped forward. He was older than the other two and should have known better. Furthermore, he was in an examination class. He was too tall to kneel on the small stool and hold it as well. It was awkward for their mother to smack him. Baby and Mato burst out laughing, which did not help their situation as Mellie only got more upset. She asked them to wash and put on their school uniform. It was one-thirty in the afternoon! She told them that they were going to school. What they had not known was that their mom had passed at school that morning to visit them but the teachers had said none of them had been in school that day. Therefore, she walked home, knowing they would be home. Mellie often went to the school in her moments off to check on her children. Baby should have known. Baby loved the moments when she saw her mother outside the school windows heading towards her. How unlucky!

Accordingly, Baby, Mato and Ally headed to school. By that time, the lower primary children were walking home in the scorching sun. All stared at each other and Baby's classmates called out to her. "Baby, Baby. She is with her mom! Ha! Ha! Ha! Baby, come over. Why are you coming to school at this time? We have been released to go home." As they walked down the road, the children's giggles disappeared into the distance.

They went to school and Mellie saw their class teachers. Baby was very embarrassed though not as much as her brothers. At least she would not be punished by the school teachers the following day. That was the first and last time their mom punished them. They did not miss school again unless they were unwell, not even Mato. Such was their mother's character, peaceful, treating her children as adults. Similar to adults, all that concerned her children was important to her. Her children learned to take responsibility for their life; as there was no adult with them a lot of the time to tell them what to do.

Reflection Time: Truancy

How does the absence of parents affect children?
When parents are absent at work or for other reasons, children may not understand.
Some parents complain that their children never take care of them. They don't understand because they sacrificed for them. Onlookers like neighbors may not get it either.
Can this absence earlier on in life make grown-up children not to visit or be there for their old and frail parents?

As a working parent, do you create time to be with your children and be part of what they are experiencing in their lives?
Many children have engaged in drugs and other substances as they look for attention from their parents who are too busy looking for money. Sometimes the most valuable gifts do not need money to buy!

~CHAPTER ELEVEN~

SELF-DOUBT

Self-doubt is highly reinforced by the continuous internal chat. This is normally negative with an internal voice repeating how inadequate one is. Based on what one has experienced through those who raised them up, the voices come from within to feed us repetitively with our unworthiness. Most of these are false.

It takes a stronger will to counter this negative voice within. The inner critic makes someone devalue their abilities, fail to cultivate their talents and look down on themselves. They fall into the temptation of comparing themselves with others.

As Baby grew up she continued to doubt herself. She felt as though she was getting smaller and smaller. A fading belief held itself in the back of her mind that she was meant for more, that she was capable of more. But life slowly began to cover it up.

The inner critic always says
'Who do you think you are?'
'You are not worth listening to'
'You are young; a woman'
If you love, you will be betrayed
Trust no-one or you'll be abandoned
If you care for anyone
You are not safe.

There were two voices within Baby. The first kept her feeling small and quiet dressed in a big jacket of fear. The other hardly audible told her she had the strength within her and that she would overcome. But this voice was small and waning.

One day, it was no day in particular and truth be told it was many one days, she said enough was enough. The negative voice had its time in the sun but things needed to change. Life seemed empty, worthless and hopeless. But she knew she had the power to change. Living under the critic's voice was no way to live. She knew she had the power to change but she needed help in getting her life back together. Thus, she demanded to the critic:

Listen to me for I have
Heard enough of your speaking
I believed you but not anymore
I no longer feel you in my core

I am more
I am going to give myself
Safety, love, trust, worth
I am going to be fully who I am meant to be

Enough, enough of giving my power away to you
I will not have any more delay
This is the only time; I'm going to be
All my bells are chiming now

I'm brave enough to journey
To make this inward journey on bended knee
Scary though it is,
I'm finding the true, long-hidden beauty

This was the fight Baby would continue to have throughout her entire life. It was the duel within her mind of the life-giver and the life-taker.

Reflection Time: Inner critic

What are your gifts?

What unique message did you come into the world to bring?

What do you need to do to reconnect with yourself and carry out that mission?

What negative messages do you harbor inside that keep you stagnated and demotivated in life.

~CHAPTER TWELVE~
VALUES

What family values hold your family of origin together?
How committedly do you need to work at your marriage to make it to work?
What can you bear or not in the marriage contract?

Mellie's children did well in school. She was the one they went to when life got tough. They knew deep within that she was the best of all the mothers on earth. She had no expectations from any of her children except her passion that they get an education. She encouraged them to do their best in school. Life had been tough for her and she wanted the best for her children.

She had a unique way of speaking. The expression she used when she wanted to say that she had no idea about anything was, 'we! Ndimanya mbiti mukamo', which directly translated to (I do not know about the hyena's udder). This she began to use frequently as the children continued through their schooling. Another of her phrases, if she wanted to say that you are fooling her, was 'ndukangwatithye ukuta' (do not keep me holding the wall). 'Naakola iyonea ta kikililo' (I have seen a lot like an entrance) she said when something was shocking).

As things got better in the family, Mellie and her children began to relax more. They smiled more and Mellie rediscovered that which she had forgotten long ago, that she had a hearty laugh. All would sit around late at night talking and laughing and telling stories.

Baby remembered a story Mellie would tell them. The story was about the bat and why it lands upside down. It went like this:

Once upon a time, there was a diarrhea outbreak in the bird kingdom. Lots of bats were affected and many died as a result. Having looked everywhere for a cure without finding one, the bats became desperate and turned to their last resort. This last resort was a curer, or a healer, who lived at the end of nowhere. The few bats that had survived flew night and day till they arrived at the healer's dwelling. The healer picked some herbs and made a syrup which they gave to the bats to drink. Along with this, she recommended that the bats sleep upside down, thus stopping the diarrhea from escaping.

Her children would scrunch up their noses and laugh. 'Ewww!' they would say as they figured out why the bats slept upside down. Mellie raised her kids on her own. Even when Fredrick was there, which was again just occasionally, it was Mellie alone who raised her children. She dared to be different and countercultural. She used her intelligence and power. She was a very strong-willed woman who taught her children by being what she wanted them to be. She was a faithful woman, sometimes to a fault. Baby would ask her at times, "Mummy why did you not marry another man, we would have had a better dad?"

To this, she would reply that daddies are given by God and that they got married in the holy church and so they were joined for life. "This is your father," she would say.

Even when Fredrick did not pull his weight in contributing towards his family's welfare, she still insisted, "He is your dad. God gave him to me".

It was a bitter truth for her to face!

Every woman was supposed to depend on her husband. No woman in Mellie's village and surrounding area except herself earned a wage. She was beyond her time in foresight. The general line of thought was that a girl's destination was marriage and there was no need to educate girls. Once married, their husbands would provide for them. In the bitter irony of the situation, it was Fredrick's absence, his trouble with drink, which had forced her to change and made her expand her possibilities.

This man she refused to leave was the reason for her independence and broadmindedness.

Despite her learning and expanded understanding of the world, she was a person excessively gentle and peaceful. When there was conflict, she could not cope. This was the school where Baby learned how to cope with conflict – to simply lose your tongue and withdraw. She preached that the family was to live in peace. When the conflict was unavoidable, as it sometimes is in life, she advised the younger one in that conflictual situation to give in.

For it was a case of respect. She always preached that the elders were to be respected even if the elder siblings were obviously in the wrong. Her children would complain, "But mom, he does this and that. It is unfair!" Mellie would respond, "Yes, but you ought to respect your elder siblings." It is needless to say, but this did not sit comfortably with those on the younger side of the age! "Christians should bear all, quietly and patiently like Mary Mother of God did." This was not always easy.

Reflection Time: Family Values

For Mellie, it was her language and storytelling to her children that created the point of connection with them. This created that magic moment when they would just laugh and be present no matter what else was happening.

For the married, how faithful are you to your partner?

We need to remind ourselves that any commitments we vow to God hold even in the midst of difficulties. There are people who can help us especially when the going gets tough, you do not need to be 'strong' or die holding it together on your own.

Identify three people you can talk to when you need encouragement.

~CHAPTER THIRTEEN~
BABY'S EXPERIENCE OF GUY

The teenage stage is critical for any youngster growing up. This is the stage between childhood and adulthood. The individual struggles at times to be a child and at other times wants to be treated like a grown-up.

At this stage, they struggle with dependence and independence. They want to push boundaries and so they need to have a firm and a loving authority figure on the other side of the wall. This helps to provide the resistance they so much need which helps them get a sense of where their power extends to.

When Baby was in her early teenage years, Guy came home. As Baby was growing up, every other person was either aunty or uncle. It took Baby some time for her to make out who Guy was to her.

Guy had come with her first-born son Bon and her two small children, one aged two and the other only a few months old. Bon was near Baby in age. When Guy's marriage had become unbearable for her, marred with all kinds of violence and torture, she left her husband and went back to Mellie. In this way, she was different from her mother.

For Baby, this was all very confusing; she did not know what was happening.

This big sister of mine came the other day. I did not know her as she was married long ago and we have never met. She is classy and I am proud to be associated with her. It seemed alright at first but it is like she is going to stay. She makes lots of knitted items like I have never seen in my life. I tell you! She is very tough. I am jealous of her depending on our mom, more mouths to feed.

Oh! My freedom is curtailed. I can no longer live freely; I cannot do or not do things when I decide and how I want. While I enjoy showing off my nephews to others, it is work for me. I have to clean and wash them. I hate this. Do you know what else I hate? I go to fetch water two kilometers away. It is a lonely path I follow. All the animals I am scared of seem to be along that path

My sister never goes to the river and I do not think she has any idea of how tiring this is. My brothers used to fetch the water before she came, but now, they only do so once in a blue moon when mom is around. When I was younger, I wanted so much to accompany them to the river but now that I am bigger I wish I could stay at home! You know water is never enough in our home anymore. It is like putting it in an anthill – it never fills. I find this the most tiring chore.

I have to cook again. I hate this too. I had to cook when Fredrick was here and I hated it then. I hate the firewood smoke! Your nose is running, your stinging beetroot red eyes are tearing and it is like you cannot breathe. When I grow up I will never use firewood!

And now that Guy is here I have to share my mom. She is hardly here as it is! I do all the chores and Guy spends all the time with mom. Nowadays when she comes home I do not even have access to her anymore. It is worse than before. She has too many people who want a piece of her, so I have given up trying to get her attention and love. After all, I do not need anybody. Not even her. I am forgotten again.

It is like I do not exist and I have no needs. I hide my needs; I do not have any anymore. Other people's needs are more important. I do not matter. The last born never matters. I feel sad inside. I am nobody. I feel lost. I feel lonely and I just work and work but will anybody see me? This is my new motto of coping with this difficult situation. My sister never talks to me.

I do not know how else big sisters relate to their younger sisters. I wish she had not come back. I fear her and do not know what to do when near her. She does not talk to me at all which suits me but it is too much. I avoid her like a plague. She is a woman I do not understand at all. You know when the older siblings are there, they seem to relate well. We are strangers to each other. I am safer alone in my room!

One day, not too long after Guy arrived, Baby was in the last class of the day in primary school, when she got up from her seat and found her dress all wet. It was wet with blood. Baby panicked. What had happened to her? She was shocked beyond belief. She did not feel unwell though she was all wet. The teacher asked two other girls in class to take her home. They never talked about what was 'ailing' her on the way. On reaching home, the girls went back and she was left with Guy who just told her, "Take that and put it on".

Baby did not know what she meant. 'Where?' she asked but Guy did not talk to her again. Baby started her novena that day. She prayed that she would be barren. Girls in school had shared that barren women never have periods. It somehow worked. She did not get periods again until after two years. She was as happy as a lark. By that time, she had learned how to deal with it in more depth.

But meanwhile,

To my sister, I do not exist. Today I have come home from school. I have started bleeding. I am in so much shock when I discover bloodstain on my uniform. I start shaking as blood means there is something very serious happening! But what hurt me? I did not feel any pain. I am in tears as I feel pity for myself. The bigger girls have taken me to the teacher who ordered them to take me home. I do not know why they are taking me home. I begin to limp.

Neither the teacher nor the girls mention what is worrying me to death. I do not even know where it comes from. I have come home to my sister and the girls have left. I am afraid. What will I tell her? The girls tell her they were asked to escort me home as I am bleeding. I start shaking at both the thought of being this sick and facing Guy. She orders me in and says 'there' and throws something to me. I take it and look at her blankly. What is this? What do I do with it? Am I dying? Can somebody please tell me?

Do I go to the hospital before I die so this bleeding may be stopped? I wish somebody can talk to me. Please, somebody, talk to me. I am scared. I do not know what to do. I am too afraid of you to ask. I need you to talk to me. Please see me, be nice to me, I feel unsure when you treat me this way.

I feel like a thing and wish you left me alone. Why did you come into my space? This is my home. I am so sad that you won't talk to me. What did I ever do to you? I had never seen you before you turned up. It was my father and now it is you. I am tired of being controlled. I am not enough for the two of you to overpower. Why won't you leave me alone?

After what appeared ages and with her heart pounding so hard she thought Guy could hear it, she asked like a scared mouse. "P...l...e...a...s...e, help me! W...h...e...re do I take this, p...l...e...a...s...e? I do not know what to do."

Guy retorted, not even lifting her head from her item. She continued to crotchet as if nothing demanded her attention. "Wherever the blood is coming from," she said simply. Baby had not known wherever it had been flowing from. She learned! That was her experience of becoming a woman.

The girls in school told me that I have joined the club. I asked them what this means and they said for the rest of my life I will get this on a monthly basis. Oh! How I hate these words! How will I manage surely? I wish I were a man. I do not like this burden of being a woman. The girls have also said the barren women do not get periods. I want so badly to be barren. I have started a novena towards praying for a miracle. Last night I even thought, God would not be so unfair as to let it come during the night! I was of course in for a rude shock!

What I am afraid of is that Guy might beat me up. That is not such a big deal but I am wondering; what may happen to me if I cannot cope anymore? I worry about myself. I feel stuck with her and do not know for how long. This home is taking my energy away. I cannot do what I enjoy doing nor do I have my freedom to do what I like whenever I like. I am just tired of being in this stuck place. I cannot talk to Guy since she won't talk to me and that worries me. I have to wait until she approaches me first. I do not like being here with her. I would like my mother back. I feel my life is threatened but I do not know what I want to do. I live every day at a time.

I feel smaller and smaller and unable to do anything for myself and must depend on others to do something for me. If I had a choice I would get someone more powerful than her to protect me. That feels safe. Yes, someone big and strong and powerful to build a very high wall around me so that I cannot even be touched by her aura. I will stay in this wall which is so high she cannot even see me. This wall is a good idea and feels very safe. I feel that I can breathe and do the little things that I like and that I enjoy. I will protect myself this way.

Since there had been no adult to monitor them for a long time, Guy thought her young siblings were spoilt brats. She felt she had to put things right by taking over the running of the home with an iron fist. This running of the home with an iron fist comprised of the beating of her siblings and her eldest born son, Bon. Bon was conceived before her marriage and she believed the failure of her marriage was his fault. She believed her husband's anger and abuse stemmed from his hatred of Bon.

Like prisoners enslaved by a brutal warden, they would whisper in the compound and make signs in order to alert each other to her presence or her whereabouts. Guy became the name no one else knew anything about except these two. It was like a type of Morse code. There was no breathing space except when she was gone to the nearby town. And when she was away, for those blissful moments they would pray that she stayed away for as long as possible, or even didn't come back.

Of course, she always came back. There was never an excuse for lazing about or for not doing one's chores. Every day before going to school, they worked on the farm or fetched water from the river. If they weren't working for Mellie's brother, who was still ordering them to do various jobs, they were working for Guy. Digging pits for banana plants was another favorite of the chores to give Baby and Bon. There was no time to play so they scheduled playtime within their chores. When they were sent on errands, they flew in order to get time to play when they got to their destination. The length of the play depended on how much time they had saved.

The other option was to play on the way, like if they were on their way to the river. They would kick the ball to each other until they reached the river; though they would have to keep clear of the sand which may give them away if found on their heads or on other parts of the body. The only game they could play in the sand was the high-jump game, seeing who could jump over the biggest obstacle and then they would have to remember to clean their legs afterwards. When Guy was at home they preferred to be away. They avoided crossing her path like a line of red fire ants. They couldn't afford to make her mad; she may easily use whatever was within her reach to beat them. They studied her and checked out for any sign of unhappiness or disappointment in her. If any of these signs were seen, Baby and Bon would flee. Mato and Ally felt less of the wrath of Guy because they were older and were able to rebel in their own ways. They would just disappear. And when they did, instead of taking her anger out on them, she took it out on Baby and Bon.

One thing Baby knew for sure was that it did not feel nice to be the last born and a girl for that matter. She felt at a great disadvantage, being a girl. She felt her options were very limited as compared with her brothers. She wished many a time that she were a boy; if she were a boy she would be able to run far away.

But at least she was not Bon, Guy's own child, for he got the brunt of her anger and punishment.

One day Guy beat her son so much that he ran away. He was eleven years old at the time. He never came back. Years later, when Guy died, he did not attend the funeral. Nothing was heard of him until Baby managed to track him down later in her life.

As quickly as Bon arrived he was gone; Baby was all alone again. With Guy's son gone, Baby had to mind Guy's two young children on her own. If any of them cried or said they had been hurt, there would be war.

When her nephew ran away, Baby was very disturbed. All focus would now be on her.

Why did you leave me alone to go through this on my own? It has been good to share in the suffering. I did not know you were going. Are you such a coward? I know it has been tough and unbearable. I just feel somehow let down but I do understand. You have done what I have no courage to do. I wish I were a boy!

Baby was not the type to run away. She would persevere no matter what. Why she did not know, but she was a fighter unknown to herself at that age. She faced every difficult situation head-on. She knew the only way through was to actually go through it.

Thus, head down and trying to avoid conflict as best she could, Baby stayed. The boys in the house often went away. They could hardly cope when life was difficult and unbearable. Perseverance was born of will, something Baby learned and came to value later in life.

When Bon ran away, he had received a nasty whipping from his mother. His back was all marked with some healing and some fresh whip marks. It was a saddening and terribly inhuman sight. Anyone who saw this eleven-year-old boy must have been moved to pity and wondered what his mother was going through to be able to do such a heinous act on her own blood and flesh. At least that was what Baby hoped as she thought about the journey Bon was now taking alone.

Baby missed him and felt betrayed by him at the same time. There would be no one else to share her story or her pain. It would really be lonely with him gone. They understood each other well and only they knew what being a child in that home meant. Baby felt helpless. Bon was never mentioned again in the house. Life continued as usual.

She had tried to persuade Bon to hang in there but he had given up hope. Nothing seemed to hold him anymore. She pleaded with him to do what she knew best – stay. But staying was not an option at all. Baby felt a failure and blamed herself for her nephew's leaving. She often wished she had courage enough to run away too. How she wished she was a boy! Because boys did what they liked, whenever they liked! This was a time when she lived in fear. She never knew what was coming and the best way to live in this situation was to keep away from trouble, though it did not always keep away from her. Her senses were highly sharpened and she was always reading Guy's face to guess what to expect. She felt suffocated and mistrustful.

Reflection Time: Identity Crisis

Guy provides a rather overpowering force which scares Baby and makes her fearful. Baby does not get the positive mentoring she so much needs as a youth growing up and struggling with all the bodily changes she is presently experiencing.

A mentor assures the teenager that the physical changes she/ he experiences are normal and that they are ok.

How do you prepare your youngsters as they grow?
How can you mentor them and reassure them as they grow?

Who are the children born out of 'wedlock', who are the excluded children or members of your family?

What would you need to do to bring them into your life?

What would it take for you to take responsibility for a child or children you have fathered even if no one else knows?

~CHAPTER FOURTEEN~
HELL SCHOOL!

In the African Culture, physical punishment was socially acceptable. In the Kamba culture as in others, a child belonged to the whole community and it was not strange for an elder in the village to scold or punish a youngster when they were found misbehaving.

Corporal punishment was used in the past both at home and in institutions and many people experienced the negative side of it. There are still those who consider it as the only way of keeping the young in the right path.

In time Baby moved on from class seven to class eight by now she was fifteen. Now she had homework and with so many chores at home, she found it difficult to do that homework. The day's chores would tire her out. But if the homework was not done, there would be serious caning at school the next day. For her morning chores, she fetched water making her the last pupil to get to school and to her class.

Her teachers never listened to any excuse whatsoever. They did what they knew best; they caned. There was no one to listen to Baby either at home or at school. Many a morning she would see one of her teachers as she fetched water from the river. It was then reported to the teacher on duty that Baby was going to be late. No matter what, she did not escape punishment.

The irony of it was that her home was so near the school they could hear the bell being rung every morning.

Sometimes, when Baby was really late and when she couldn't bear the punishment, she would hide in the protestant church midway between her house and the school. The church was thatched with iron sheets that had become rusty over time. The floor was earthen and was always dry and easy to draw images or write on. Even when it rained, the church remained dry and dusty. The seats were made by sticking planks of wood into the floor and then laying straight pieces of sisal poles across them. They weren't comfortable

The church had two-door holes, one at the back and one at the front, left side. Baby would always come in through the front, left side as that was closest to the road. It wasn't a big church, about twenty by eight meters. Two windows opened on each side and let in some light. There were no glass panes or blinds and though nobody attended church on any day other than Sunday, Baby would still have to hide in one of the two corners to not be visible to passers-by.

Business here in this house is not as usual. I do not know who to turn to. You do not see or listen to me. Are you afraid of her too? I am sick of everything and all of you adults without spines. I am angry and sad at myself for being so much a coward that I cannot run away so you all can see how serious this is. I am a spineless little hare as well.

Mother, please tell me where you are when all this is happening to me. Why have you left Guy to torture us without your intervention? Whenever we tell you we are not happy you only say that we are the younger ones and we should respect her. It hurts. Can you not see that I am not happy anymore? When I talk to you, I do not feel listened to. Why do you not listen to me, mother? It is hell in this home and I wish I could leave. You just keep quiet like things are usual.

In order to successfully sail through primary school education, an exam had to be taken. This exam cost some money and by the time Baby was ready to take her exam she had caught up with her brother, Mato. Both should have sat exams that year but Mellie could not afford to have two children joining secondary school. So, because it was feared that Mato would not complete his education if he was asked to repeat, he took the exams and Baby was set back two years, having to retake the classes which led to the exams.

It was a blessing in disguise. This school was a better school. In this school she had a new start. No other children from her village attended this school and the teachers were as new to her as she was to them. There were no preconceived ideas about who she was or what her past held. She was a new person, a blank slate.

Baby passed her exams with flying colors and got admitted to an all-girls' school.

Reflection Time: School Experience

Is caning the only means to make a child obedient?

What other alternatives are there for parents or teachers to use to train their children in keeping the law?

Maya Angelou said people do the best they know how until they know better and when they know better they do better. If some of these beliefs do not serve us today and the consequences on our children are dire, how can we influence the young differently? This would reduce the pain in the world.

Does any child go to school late for no reason?

Notice how Baby gets punished at school because the teachers made certain assumptions about her attending school late.

As a teacher, should you take time to actually find out why a child could be regularly coming late?

Can adults wait long enough for the child to say actually what is bothering them?

There are many children we know from our school days and possibly later who dropped out of school for fear of punishment at home or at school. Had Baby not had a caring mother who followed up, she may have dropped out.

~CHAPTER FIFTEEN~ SECONDARY NAVIGATION

When we see unusual behavior in young children or teenagers are we keen enough to find out what is changing?

When teenagers do not have the skills to cope with changes either in their lives or changes that affect their loved ones it can be stressful.

It takes the intervention of a caring adult either at home or in school to prevent a disaster.

The new school Baby went to was an all-girls school, a rarity at the time as the education of girls was seen as a suspicious endeavor. It was a safe place for those girls willing and able to study and it stood as a symbol of the strength of the missionary effort to educate girls.

It was a sign of success and courage. It provided answers to questions like were girls as intelligent as boys? Could a girl be trusted to complete school or would a parent be disappointed midway as a girl dropped out due to unexpected pregnancy? This place was an answer to those questions. It was a center of excellence and throughout the region, stories were heard of girls from that school who had succeeded in life. It gave young women a nearly automatic hope of doing well in life through good education.

The school was built on a hill. It was called Kiimani, literally meaning the school on the hill. The terrain was rocky and uneven and the students during break time would bask in the sun on the rocks, enjoying the sun and the freedom of not being stuck indoors. Interspersed among the rocks and on top of the hill were the occasional trees and grassy areas. These provided shelter and a nice breeze during the hot, dry season.

Run by Irish nuns, the teachers and workers were very friendly, focused and encouraging. Everyone worked as a team. Students were gently encouraged to do better, to be better. A school such as this was a very long-awaited gift for Baby.

It was an escape from home. It would be another three months before the school break.

There were always chores, always work, to be done at home. Amazingly endless chores. She never had the time to study. Now she was off to boarding school. Whatever chores awaited her at school were nothing compared to what she had done at home.

Time flew by at this new school. While there were the standard issues every person faced as they passed through the school, the time itself was uneventful. The only really important event was just over a year after Baby started. Mellie became too old to work and had to retire at 55. For years she had toiled and worked, back bent, with little reward for her labor. She never dreamed of being able one day to actually retire. Yet now this day was upon her.

Just when Baby was settling to being with her.

She was thanked for the work she had done at the school and sent home with some little money, a wheelbarrow and a 'panga' (a machete used for cutting wood and sometimes grass). The money she deposited in a postal account she had had for some years now and the wheelbarrow and panga went home with her. Though she was retired, she would still work, now becoming a full-time farmer. Perhaps there was no rest after all.

And Baby again was left alone.

This is where life began to change for Baby. She started getting blackouts. A week never went by before she fainted again. She did not understand what was causing this. It always happened in the laboratory during the chemistry lesson. It began to happen after Mellie left, the same time as Baby started wetting her bed.

I am left alone again. I knew it would happen. Had I not been waiting for this? Mom is gone again. I knew all the time she would not stay with me. So, she went. Oh! How it hurts. I cannot cope with school. I am much disturbed, though I do not fully know what these feelings mean. I feel alone. How will I cope without you near me? This time at school was the longest time I have been near you but it was not enough. I want a lifetime. I want the time that was lost to me when I was growing up.

I begin to drop in school. I do not know how to readjust. I get blackouts. I go to the lab and as soon as I smell those chemicals, I just pass out. I wish I knew what is happening to me. That is part of the problem. I have to continue with my studies. I do not feel like I have a choice. Again, the teachers here cannot help me.

I do not talk to anyone even though I am struggling. I feel I cannot trust anyone. Besides, what do I talk about when I do not even know what is happening to me? I retreat into a world of my own. No one even imagines mom's retirement has affected me; sure, I should be a big girl.

I have been left again. No one cares how I feel. My mum still has to go and she is gone. I find it hard to manage. I do not even know what coping is. I am here again in a boarding school. I wish I had not come here in the first place. I do not know what is happening in my body.

I am scared silly of this chemistry teacher. She is very familiar. I know what I feel towards her from somewhere. She behaves like my sister and I cannot bear this anymore. She is as tough as leather. She scares the life out of me and I cannot understand her subject. I am frustrated I do not understand. Before I know it I black out. This is the only way I know how to respond.

Mum is not here and it is lonely here. I am scared of being without her. I feel abandoned and in darkness. School feels too long and I should be out of here. I do not like wetting my bed. I have started doing that and it is frustrating. I do not like it because I know I should not be. I feel ashamed of it. Others do not understand how hard I try not to. I do not like this feeling of being unable to stop. Sometimes I even stay up as long as possible so that I have shorter nights but I still do. I have avoided drinks at night and this still does not work. Tell me this is not about drinks and length of night and I believe you.

I feel very embarrassed when I find my bed wet every morning. I even fear going to bed. At times I have to wait until everyone has gone to bed before I can retire. I keep shifting from side to side to the drier part of my bed. The more I get worried about it the more I do it. It is very frustrating. I wish I could change this. How I wish other girls knew how difficult it is for me at this time. I hate it when people bring up this topic on bedwetting. I wish I knew what to do about it.

Then I have started fainting. It happens when I go to the lab. I just feel dizzy and before I know It I am on the ground. It is a real blackout since all I see is blackness. I seem to go to my own world where I do not see or hear. I seem to be gone for ages and when I come back, these girls are surrounding me. This too makes me embarrassed. I do not know what to say to them. I find it hard not to know why or what is happening in my own body.

It was not an easy time for Baby, the months between when her mother left and when she sat for her exams. But as with everything in Baby's life, this too began to pass and four years after Baby started at the new girls' school, at the age of 19, Baby sat for her exams.

I have always been known by the name Baby but I have been asked in preparation for this exam to give my full name. I need another name to make three including my surname. I have enquired if I had another name and they tell me that my other name is 'Mutheu'. This is my grandmother's name on my father's side. I am not sure I like that name. I feel no connection with it.

My grandmother died before I was born. I do not know her and no one talks about her. I am not too keen on connecting with her. My other name is Esther. This is the grandmother on my mom's side. She is dead too but there is more warmth surrounding her. She nearly became a traditional healer, you know – those who would connect with the spirits! This is what I hear about her. I like that name. My other name is Fredrick. I must take it as I exist in the patriarchal society and the father's name is always taken by each child. It comes first in the list in fact.

Fredrick Esther Mutheu. That is my name. But it is also not my name. My name is Baby. I am forever called Baby.

Baby sailed through her exams and passed with high marks. Now she was finished and could explore her options. Her original plan was to be a nurse but she did a few interviews for medical training and quickly realized she didn't like that. Her elder brother who was training to be a nurse had been talking about going to the morgue as part of the training and this had turned Baby off medicine completely.

As Baby decided what to do next, she lived at home, working on the farm. It was a challenge to move back in with her family after the freedom she had enjoyed at school, but it was a necessity while she decided what to do with her life. But now she was grown and there was more ease in relating at home. (She was treated with more respect as she had somehow proved her determination by completing secondary schooling. That is without pregnancy as was common with lots of girls then).

College was an option. Application season was ending soon so she would have to decide. But she didn't really know what she wanted to study.

Every year there was a women's meeting at the Diocese. It was something Baby knew about because of her continued attendance at church but she had never gone. Fredrick did not approve of paying for his daughter – who should be learning to cook and clean – to attend a 'festival for women'. This year, as Baby and Mellie sat side by side, four pews in and slightly to the left of center, the announcement was again made for the coming meeting. This year would see a series of formative seminars and discussions, all led by prominent women within the churches. Baby squirmed in her seat as her frustration grew. Should she even bother asking?

After church ended and the long conversations drew to a close, Mellie and Baby made their way home. She had to ask. It was too big of an opportunity to let pass. Maybe he would change his mind. By the time she had formulated a winning argument within her mind, they had arrived home. Fredrick was sitting under the shade of the house, uncomfortable at their having gone to church at all.

Baby called the attention of Fredrick and attempting to be as formal as her stomach would allow her to be though it twisted within her at the thought of showing him respect. "May I…."

"Let me, Baby." It was Mellie. "Go and bring us some tea."

"What is happening?" He enquired. (Fredrick had crossed his legs and swung one impatiently. He often did this when he was in deep thought).

"We have exciting news. Our priest is paying for some of the most active members of the church to attend the women's meeting and they have picked Baby and me. It is a huge honor for the whole family and everyone is talking about it."

Baby went in and brought the aluminum teapot and two mugs, one for each parent and served it together with the scones. She walked away, half-listening to catch Fredrick's response.

Fredrick looked indifferent but said nothing. Mellie had checkmated him. Later that night, when Fredrick left to find the drink, Mellie told Baby that she would pay for both of them to go. She knew Baby wanted badly to attend and Fredrick wouldn't let her. So, this time both would go under the pretense of getting a personal invite from the priest.

Baby was ecstatic. Two weeks later they journeyed to the meeting. Baby met other Christian women her age. She met women who thought like her and asked the questions she asked. Discussions were held on faith, vocation, growth and development, everything that Baby had wanted to discuss. She had found others like her.

Baby also met the nuns.

Mellie was a long-term employee of the Irish nuns during her years at the school. Baby had a fair amount of experience with the nuns from her time as a student. But now Baby was an adult, she had graduated, no longer the student. Even before her time with the nuns, Baby had known of them from the times they visited her mother. Always dressed in bright white, they were kind and loving. Baby had for many years toyed with the idea of joining their ranks. That way she could use her gifts and skills to help those in need, to help the poor and the orphaned.

Baby remembered when she was a child when the nuns came to visit. Everybody loved the nuns. They were very well respected. It was such a privilege to have the nuns in their home. In Kamba tradition, an honored guest was offered gifts when they leave as a thank you. Baby remembered the nuns receiving amazing gifts from her mother. Eggs, oranges or vegetables. There was always a chicken that had been fattened specifically to give to the nuns. Nobody else could slaughter that chicken.

When Baby and Mellie returned from the meeting, Baby said little about the nuns. She applied for college and got back to work on the farm. All she did was send a letter to the nuns thanking them for their conversation during the meeting and letting them know that she was interested in possibly joining, but that she also wanted to go to college to become a teacher. She had only realized she wanted to become a teacher during the journey back from the meeting, in the hotly crowded bus as it kicked up dust on the bumpy road.

A week later a reply came. This was the first piece of mail Baby had ever received and her excitement was enormous.

The letter thanked Baby for her interest and invited her to a *Come and See*. She was elated. She read the letter over and over and placed it under her pillow. She continued reading. Was this real? Her family wanted her to go to college. Baby was over the moon!

It was two hours before anyone else returned to the house and by then Baby had relaxed. She told her mother privately but nobody else. It wasn't until after the *Come and See*, after the affirming spirit she felt as she went about the daily life of the nuns for a few days, that she made her decision and let her immediate family know.

Baby was to train to become a nun. Some siblings could not understand how she could waste a college opportunity!

Reflection Time: Stress in our lives

In spite of difficulties, individuals find a way to cope eventually. When there is an understanding adult who mentors the youngster, time is saved and energy spent trying to charter the way for oneself is used productively in studies or at work.

Some teenagers may readily find someone to talk to like a caring religious leader, parent, relative, teacher or a counsellor.

It is, however, important to realize that some youth may feel hesitant to do this and it is such who need a responsible adult to notice and invite them to share respectfully

END OF PART TWO

~CHAPTER SIXTEEN~
MELLIE IS OFF

When we do not understand painful situations in our lives we look for ways to make sense of them. We seek to find the origin of the pain. The Kamba people take this seriously as they believe every situation has a cause. HIV was and still is a cause of question and deep searching for many individuals, families and cultures.

In the months leading up to Baby's initiation into the convent, she decided to travel to visit the family she knew she had but had never met. Most of her family lived by the Kenyan coast, where business was thriving and a well-educated individual could make a living – Mellie had made sure her children were well-educated.

She visited her brothers. Loki, whom she knew little about because he left when she was still young and Ally, who she had not seen for many years. Mulili also lived at the coast but she did not get to see him. Baby also visited her sister, Guy, who had moved to the coast and had got a job working in the business. Baby was a bit hesitant when it came to Guy but was pleasantly surprised. For the first time, Baby was treated by Guy as an adult.

I have never been to the coast, never seen the sea in my life. The heat is actually killing, it is so hard to inhale. But it is a break from hard work at home. Guy does not belittle me which is very surprising. I thought it would be excruciating but to her, I am now a grownup. It is exciting being a grownup. I like visiting my brother Loki too. He loves me very much and it is nice to get to know him. He treats me like his young sister. I really like this. It makes me feel very appreciated and loved.

My brother Loki has this very sore spot on his back, somewhere below his shoulder. He is in so much pain he sheds tears. He cannot reach his wound so he asks me to clean it for him. He is my brother but it is gross. I clean his wound and prepare breakfast. He is in so much pain he cannot eat most of the mealtimes. Loki is sore. Whenever he wears a shirt it sticks on to his wound and it would make you cry as you pull it out of the fresh skin. I do not like seeing people I love suffer. I wish I could reduce his pain. I use saline water. I ask him to go to the hospital but they have told him that they cannot do anything for him. I feel helpless. I have heard rumors about a certain disease called HIV/AIDS which our teacher in the school has told us to be careful of. This is my brother. I refuse to associate him with such a disease. I push those thoughts out of my mind and think I should pray for him. As I leave for home, he tells me to ask our mother to pray for him.

Two weeks after getting back from the coast, Baby started her training to become a nun and her life was consumed by all the training and work she had to do, not to mention her studies. Life soon crowded out the growing situation at the coast.

Over the years, Mellie had pleaded with her stepbrother to sell her the two acres of land she had lived on. Most of her children had by now moved on but she still opened her home to the children of friends and family who needed somewhere to live. Life was still unknown on that land and she hoped he would relent and sell it to her. Surely her own stepbrother would not send her away. The older people were by that time very attached to their land and did not sell land easily, but she thought having lived on that land for so long, he would eventually sell it to her. She always shopped for her stepbrother and gave him money whenever he needed it. And her sons were always available to work the land when needed. After all, he had more than he needed.

Then one day, her brother's son came home. He had lived far away and had just sold his own land. The money he got from that land was given to his father and immediately his father gave it to Mellie. It was a refund for all the work and money Mellie and her children had given him over the years. It was a payment. It meant he was never going to sell. It was a hot day, that day and Mellie was seated in the shade of the jacaranda tree when he came to visit. As was the custom, the older person was always first to greet the younger so he uttered the customary 'Wakya Mellie' and then sat down. He received a cup of tea and a meal, as was also custom. It was a soft meal for he had few teeth and, except for meat – even the toothless had meat - even if he could not chew well. When he had eaten to his fill, he got into the business. He silently handed over the money and without saying any more than he needed to, told her what it was for.

Mellie was shocked and immensely disappointed. She needed land and he was her only hope. It seems she was to retire with no stable home, no security and...

Suddenly, Mellie panicked. She was afraid. She knew Fredrick would soon know about the money. Now he was away at the nearby town. It would not be long before he was back again and when he learned about this great sum he would demand it and disappear into a drinking frenzy. This was too big a sum to be blown on drink.

She thought of depositing the money in the postal account but that would not guarantee its safety. Mellie watched her stepbrother disappear into the forest, looking but not thinking about him. Her mind was racing to find a solution. As she got up from her seat by the tree she got an idea! Two of her children lived on the Kenyan Coast. She could travel there. It was a sudden decision and though it didn't guarantee the money's safety forever, it was a start.

For fear that Fredrick would arrive soon, she decided to leave the very next morning. She made the preparations. Her nerves kept her awake the whole night but ultimately the sun began to rise. At dawn she left home, feigning a trip to the market. She was so afraid of her husband that she continuously looked over her shoulders, thinking he was following her.

Just like those years before when she fled his rage, she decided to walk instead of boarding the bus. A bus was too risky, for he might follow and there were many who could tell him where she went.

At the time the nearest tarmacked road was over forty kilometers away and it was that road Mellie needed to get to. The railway line ran adjacent to that road. Once there she could get the train the rest of the way. Reaching this point as quickly as possible was her only goal, moving as far away from Fredrick before her absence raised his curiosity.

She left home on Friday morning – market day – carrying her kiondo, as she always did on market day. She looked normal, save for that her pace was slightly quickened. What no onlooker could tell, however, was that she had stored a few clothes and the money in the kiondo, nicely covered up and concealed.

It was cultural for people to exchange some pleasantries when they met on the roads during their journey. They would chat about their business and where they were going. Any unanswered, or ill-answered question could be repeated for more information. Everybody she met before she reached the market required no further questions for it was obvious that she was going to the market, but once she had reached and passed the market the questions became harder to answer satisfactorily and she found herself lowering her eyes so as not to engage with others. It was hardly inconspicuous but it was all she could do.

As she walked, she also avoided the roads and walked through smaller pathways. She was aware that, in case Fredrick suspected she had left and had given chase, she would be easier to track down if she were along the main path. So, she opted for the dusty lonely side roads and paths. Here, homes were kilometers apart and that meant as she moved away from the more congested market areas the landscape became more isolated. She could move quicker and talk to fewer passers-by. In this way, she covered as much distance as she could.

When evening fell, she walked into the first homestead she came across. If she felt at ease in that space she would ask them to offer her a place to sleep. It was common at the time – though becoming less so due to the number of strangers moving into the area – to act kindly towards travelers. Mellie felt at peace and so the first night she stayed at the first homestead she walked into. It was a simple, welcoming homestead and Mellie found no trouble in acquiring a bed for the night. Making sure to fill up her bottle of water, she continued her journey early the next day.

The weather was hot. It was May. Rains fell in March and April and again in October, November and December. During May, the sun-dried the land and the remaining grass on the farms was scorched brown. Domestic animals grazed on dry twigs. Occasionally, whirlwinds, evidenced by the swirling red dust, moved snaking through the bare flat land. The whirlwinds could be spotted kilometers away. The sky was completely blue and offered no clouds to shade the intense heat of the sun. Even the trees offered little service, for they were bare and had shed their leaves. They had looked dried up and any shade that could be found was scattered and patch worked along the ground. Nothing happened this second day and in the evening she again walked into the first homestead she saw and asked to be put up and this too was responded to positively. When it came to women and children, people were particularly nice and would not leave them to the mercy of the dark, dry wilderness. Again, she filled up her bottle and the next morning continued her journey before dawn. Mellie was a tough woman but age was approaching her. On the third day of walking, she began to feel the effects of the dirt against her feet and the sun against her head. Her feet were beginning to burn and blister and her head was beginning to feel faint. All she could do was drink and continue, fighting through the pain. What she carried with her, the future of her family, was enough at this time to keep her going. Her hope was to catch the evening train which left for the coast by seven o'clock. As morning became noon and noon became afternoon she began to hear it. Miles away the heavy engines chugged away. It was the only evidence that she was getting closer. If she continued this pace she would make it by evening's fall.

The landscape was beginning to change slightly. The area where she walked was populated by huge Baobab trees, with branches that looked like dried roots singing praises to the sun. Many anthills scattered the land too, anthills some of which were meters high. Once in a while, she saw a herd of cattle in the uninhabited area. There were no settlements in view and she imagined this to be government land.

Suddenly a shot of adrenaline ran through Mellie's veins and fear ceased her movement. Not far in front of her was a snake's path, wound into the dirt and yet cleared by the wind. Living in a snake-infested area had forced Mellie to recognize the clues of their movement and she knew that though she couldn't see it, there was a giant snake nearby. She crossed the track in a wide arch and ran for some distance. The heat of the sun boiled her forehead as she did and soon she had to return to a walk. She took a sip of her water. Her rosary beads found their way into her hand and she began again her practice of praying and moving through the beads.

She did not stop her prayer until about five o'clock in the evening when she began to notice that she was on the outskirts of the railway station town. A shot of energy ran through her and chased the tiredness away. Finally! Then she heard the hooting of the cargo train heading towards the town. She dragged her feet a little faster.

They were burning and she was thirsty and hungry. She had descended in altitude from where she began her journey and the heat from the sun seemed to intensify as if the land trapped its warmth.

When she arrived at the station she was starving. She didn't know any of the eating places so she wandered around for a few minutes. Most restaurants were small, simple and only prepared basic foods. As Mellie walked, a colorful little house caught her eye. It looked clean and welcoming. When she walked in she asked if they could prepare ugali and goat stew with vegetables. Of course, they could. With her meal, she drunk two cups of Kenyan tea. After she ate, her energy levels rose and she went and bought her ticket.

Now she waited for the evening train. There were many travelers waiting for the train and instinctively Mellie moved closer to the women her age. Here she could blend in. It would take the slow train some time to get here so she had some time to doze. By eight-thirty the siren went and they were asked to get ready to board. At exactly nine o'clock, the train departed from the station, loaded with Mellie and many other strangers.

Her brief rest while waiting at the station did nothing to stave off Mellie's tiredness and she was so exhausted that as soon as she got to her seat she slept. It was a whole night's journey and Mellie slept the whole time. The train reached Mombasa the next morning at seven o'clock.

From here, Mellie caught a bus, travelling north. It was a three-hour journey because of the terrible road conditions but nothing of any interest happened, save for an individual halfway through attempting to enter the bus despite its already overcrowded state; full of humans and suitcases and wicker baskets and two chickens. After the bus, it was a thirty-minute walk to Guy's house. Only when she arrived did her fears of Fredrick abate. She was on high alert during the whole of the journey and even when she slept she felt as if she was watching out for Fredrick.

Though Mellie would not realize this until her return journey, she had little to worry about, for Fredrick's mind was on other things. While Mellie was making this journey in an attempt to save the money, Mellie's stepbrother's sons came to her house to say that they would not allow their father to sell that land to her. They didn't know that he had already given Mellie the money and were angry that Mellie educated all her children while their father refused to educate them. They were jealous and envious too that she did this while on their land. What they forgot was that education was investment this woman had the foresight to plan for. She believed in education and opposition did not stop her from giving it to her children. They refused to negotiate at all with Mellie's children that were left at the house and all they wanted was for her family to leave straight away. They were ready for action and they started knocking down the house and pushing the family out of the land.

At the time, Mellie was an anchor for many, five children – some grandchildren, some belonging to distant relatives – were staying with Mellie. Guy's last two children also stayed with Mellie as Guy tried her hand at some business at the coast. With Mellie away, the anchor had been swept away and her children did not know what to do. The only possible hope was for Fredrick to do something but he was away on the day the intruders came. Her children, unsure of what do to, left their properties in the various homes of those they knew. If only they had been warned, they would have been ready to go.

Before the week was over they had all reconnected with each other and with the help of good Samaritans they were able to rent a few rooms in a nearby shopping center. This shopping center had around twenty or so shops where people could buy vegetables and daily provisions. Behind these shops were built several single rooms which were rented out to tenants on a monthly basis.

But they could not afford enough rent to accommodate all of them. It was emotionally and physically unbearable for everyone to try and cram under one roof. They had nothing, for the furniture they could save was too big for this small place and had to be given to neighbors for safekeeping. With Fredrick too old to work and the children too young to work (or too busy with school), it was not a very easy time.

Like the Israelites, in the Old Testament, they began to reminiscence how life had been. They appreciated what had been! The home had been an orchard where there were all kinds of fruit in abundance. There were oranges, bananas, avocadoes and mangoes. As a sign of remorsefulness, Fredrick had settled into work on the farm around their old home. He was too old but there was no other option. Maybe it was his penance. He worked from the crack of dawn till dusk and, surprisingly, the land responded generously.

When you are meant for the farm it is difficult to cope with town life. There was no privacy, no room and they just felt out of place. They felt everyone in the village talked about them and it was hard for them to be in their neighborhood where all the talk spread like wildfire. By the time they were taking plan B to move to Fredrick's young brother's house, Mellie was due to join them.

When they moved to Fredrick's young brother's home it was not easy either. His young brother had died many years earlier. So, his wife and children found it difficult to receive them. They reminded their uncle Fredrick that he had sold his land and asked if he now wanted to possess this land too. Being very embarrassed by this way of speaking, Fredrick just kept quiet. This was not his territory and he needed their goodwill. He, therefore, had to be on his best behavior.

During all this time, Mellie was at the coast. The coast should have been a place of unwinding and holidaying. She, however, had been met by another horror of her life. Though she should have been enjoying the vastness of the ocean and basking in the warmth of the sunny beaches, she had instead become her daughter's primary caretaker. For the months while she had been living with Guy, she had been Guy's nurse. Guy was unwell. Mellie did not know what her daughter ailed from. She was unable to cope. Her stress levels were very high, so high that she was going berserk.

As mothers always do, did she know something about Guy's ailment?

Mellie's sons, Loki and Mato, also lived near the coast and they would come often to visit and help. But the help they offered was little, for they both worked and had responsibilities. Mellie was old and though she was a tank when it came to the farm, she was not built for life in the city and her health began to deteriorate. She started behaving queerly. She started walking for miles on end. She carried on her back a little boy she was very fond of. He was Peter's son, the neighbor. She was tasked to take care of him while both his parents went to work. She would carry him and walk briskly to the church, which was about three kilometers away. When she came back she would close herself in the house. She would not listen to the radio or even read or do anything.

With time she stopped going out of the house completely.

Eventually, the hair on her skin changed to grey and her skin grew pale with lack of exposure to the sun. She became more and more fearful and unbalanced. Loki and Mato were too busy to notice anything and Guy was too unwell. There was too much happening in their worlds for them to notice. Life just passed-by. Day followed night and everyone was lost in their thoughts and worries. Mellie's mind too had decided to switch off, she had gone to the world of no more feeling, the mind only allowing enough for her to survive!!

One day Baby woke up with a strange feeling. This was the first time Baby was away from home for such a length of time. She missed her family – she missed Mellie. She felt an urge to go and visit her mother, who she knew was at the coast. It was so irresistible. She had not heard from home for ages and so she did not know about the displacement of her family.

I feel as though I must go. I do not know what causes this desire to visit but I feel pulled, dragged. Is it that my mother is unwell?

I'm sure she is fine. I'm sure I just miss her. Essentially, I miss her terribly. I must go and see her. I must see if I can get time off.

Baby was only allowed three days to go to the coast and back. Every minute counted and she travelled as quickly as she could. She left excruciatingly early on her first morning off and travelled for twelve hours straight to get to the coast. By the time she got to her brothers' town, it was just after four in the evening. She went to her brother's place of work – Blue Bay Hotel – and waited for him to get off work. By this time, she was washed out and her feeling of worry was intensifying, though she didn't know why. When he got off work, they went and got a meal before heading to her sister's house. Baby was too tired and too nervous to eat. The food was tasteless. Even though she yearned for the silence, she found her brother too quiet. She started wondering what the silence was about. They did not do feelings easily in her family so she sensed that soon she would learn of some bombshell. He did not talk much so she tried asking questions in order to get her brother to talk. It didn't work.

Then suddenly, "By the way, Guy got admitted at the Coast General Hospital last week."

Baby was silent for a moment. "Why did anybody not tell me?" she then asked. Of course, that went unanswered and the silence continued for some time longer.

"How is mum?" Baby had noticed that he had said nothing about how Mellie was. Baby had not seen her mother for close to seven months - a really long time.

"She is well." More dead silence.

After they finished their dinner, they walked silently until they reached her sister's house. They stood at the door and her brother knocked. A second time. A third... the door opened slightly. All they could see was Mellie's left eye through the slit of the door. She held the door firmly from the inside. Should not Baby have smelt a rat when Mato was so low and quiet? Their mother peeped like a mouse to make sure she could trust who was standing outside the door. Then her brother told her, "Mum, it is us, Baby and I."

Silence! Loud silence! It was so loud that you could hear the hearts beating.

Baby could not comprehend this.

I know it. I knew it. But what do I know? What happened to you, my mother? You have gone but I do not know where. Somewhere I cannot connect with you. You normally greet me twice or thrice, especially when you have not seen me for a long time. You have not done that tonight and that is why I know something has happened to you. I am beginning to worry. You are whispering and asking us to do the same because there are people out there who want to get rid of us.

I have stopped talking as I do not know what to say. I feel very hurt. How can you not know it is such a long time since we saw each other? Why do you not know me? You have not asked me how life has been for all those months. I feel lost. I cannot give too much time to my feeling. I do not matter now, you do. I will do what I have always done all my life.

I am your mother now, Mellie. I am convinced that you need me now more than ever before. You look so vulnerable. I notice you have not eaten or slept for months. I have to be responsible and I will be. I am taking you back with me.

How will I be able to face the world when my mother is out of her mind? I cannot lose face. I should hold everything together. (The center must hold no matter what.) This is the time for me to be strong even though I feel like breaking down. I am tougher than this situation. Mother is talking. She is talking alone but as though she was in communication with others. "Mother, are you talking? Whom are you talking to?" This scares me all the more. I am so scared. I cannot understand. I have forgotten about the poor me whose mother does not even know I worry about mom. How will others see me when they hear that my own mother has gone insane? No way. This cannot be. Baby was so worried about other people's judgments.

Mato did not stay long. He was unable to answer any of Baby's questions and he didn't how to. Life had made Mato go into eternal silent mode – he was always known in the family for this trait but this was something else. Having said good night, he left. Baby asked him to call by the next day as she needed to visit her sister in the hospital before she left for home. Baby was too disturbed to sleep a wink that night. She sorted out her mother's clothes and packed them. Her mother talked to herself the whole night and didn't even acknowledge Baby's presence. Baby might as well have been on her own.

Early the next morning, they left for the hospital.

I have not slept the whole night. I am too worried. I cannot wait for tomorrow to move out of this place. I have never seen my sister sick. They say she is too ill to eat. I am scared, scared of what might happen. I sense something and for now, I am too numb to feel anything else but fear, which I am attempting to replace my thinking and thinking hard. I am thinking about what I need to do in two days. Toughen up is what I need to do now. I have to be tougher.

Reflection Time: Stress

What do you do when faced with difficulties in your life?

Where is God when you are experiencing suffering or life challenges?

At times like these, many people fear to ask God some hard questions.

What questions can you allow yourself to ask God right now?

You will find your relationship with God matures as a result!

~CHAPTER SEVENTEEN~
HIV/AIDS IMPACT

HIV/AIDS has affected many families in the world, especially African families. Due to HIV/AIDS, children have been orphaned too young to mind themselves, mothers have been widowed, men have lost their wives and extended families have been overwhelmed by deaths. The community and society have had to chip in to help desperate situations of dealing with orphans. There are many families that are headed by children who only have each other's shoulders to lean and keep warm on.

Mellie kept saying that her daughter Guy was dying in hospital.

But when Baby said they would go and see her, Mellie began to shake. She couldn't see her. She wouldn't. It took a lot of time and energy to convince their mother to go in and see her daughter. Mellie kept saying that she did not want to see Guy. She didn't want to see her dying daughter. But Baby wanted to see her and they could not leave Mellie like this. They could not leave a mentally disturbed woman at home, alone. When Baby reminded her that they were travelling home and might not see Guy again, she reluctantly agreed.

Mellie was right, she knew in her heart what Baby had not perceived within her mind. She was deeper in connection with another truth! Well known by her heart. It was eleven o'clock by the time they were allowed to visit the ailing sister and Mellie's second daughter. Mato and Loki were there. Mato led the way into the ward. Guy was in an isolation ward, towards the back of the hospital. The walls were all a block of dying grey concrete. The windows had thin white curtains and some had no glass. A generator was hooked up to several of the beds in case the electricity went out. This way, those on life support wouldn't die during a power outage. Mato led the way past the sick towards the sicker. In silence. Finally, he stood by a bed. When he did, Baby could easily have sworn he had made a mistake. On the bed, lay skeletons that remained of a tall strong beautiful woman - a sister she had not seen for some time. Surely it had not been that long.

Her mouth was all sores and her stare, hardly changing, was fixed on the ceiling.

“Guy! Baby, mum, Mato and I are here to see you”. Loki said, trying to sound comforting but coming across as shaky and scared. How could he not be scared? He, too, had HIV. He was showing signs of the virus before anybody knew Guy even had it. It was only the unpredictable nature of the disease that allowed Guy to get down fast. She had succumbed! Loki did not know when his time would come. Baby’s heart jerked!

Whatever remained of her sore-covered lips could not cover her teeth. She looked scary and Baby found it hard to know what to do. It was mad humid and everyone including Guy had sweat dripping down their forehead. It was hard to tell whether it was psychological or physical sweat. She struggled to turn her body. After what seemed like an eternity Guy turned her gaze to face Baby. Death turned her head slowly towards Baby

“Take me to the shower, please.”

Baby nearly died. She was scared of Guy. She knew Guy was HIV positive even though no one had told her and here she was asking to be washed.

HIV/AIDS was a relatively new disease at the time. It was the early nineties and no one dared speak about it, let alone admit that your relative had it. There were all kinds of myths about it. The patient was avoided like the plague. A person would be wrapped with a polythene bag before burial if they died of this disease. At the time there was no medicine for it so patients bore the pain and when the time came, they died.

It was still not clear if it was safe to touch or share utensils with such patients. Baby thought blood.....for better for worse. She was the only woman around who could wash her.

Baby wished someone else emotionally stronger could help her but there was no one else to turn to! If only Nduku her late sister was alive, she would have shouldered this huge responsibility!

Mellie murmured, 'I knew my 'babies' are dying.....why?'

Baby swallowed her terror and her distress, gathering all she had left together. She lifted Guy's twig arm over her head and shoulder and supported her middle back with her other arm. They walked, shakily, step by step towards the shower. They didn't talk. Guy couldn't and Baby wouldn't. While in the shower Baby stripped Guy's, hospital gown off while supporting her frail body. Guy could not stand on her own. Then she turned on the cold knob. Baby had imagined she would need a cold shower given that it was very humid. Guy began to shiver with cold. To hold it together baby bit her teeth. Her teeth cluttered loudly unable to hide it any longer. She then turned on the warm tap and within seconds, the water was warm.

Guy began to speak slowly and tiredly. "I have not had a shower for days. Whenever I ask anyone to take me, they are too busy to do so."

Most people, even the medical staff, still were not sure of how to handle patients that suffered from this disease. Any information available was scanty or fear instilling. They were all scared of contracting it themselves.

I am very scared. As she stands, I can see how frail she looks. I have shortness of breath. My sister's body is so completely wasted that she is ghostly. She is holding onto me so she does not slide and fall. I wish I were her brother and so I would not have to face this. I am shaking like a blade of grass against a whirlwind. Oh! God my heart is nearly missing a beat and my legs are wobbly. She is holding me tight. I can feel her bones. She is scary to look at. I know I have to be strong even though I am scared to near death. The nurses are exchanging glances as they let us pass. I feel angry with them. I shake because of fear of death; she shakes because of illness - the inevitable that seems so near, so close.

This was her sister for heaven's sake.

She needs care. Why would the medical staff not do something more? She says they have not been touching her much. My hands are shaking as I wash her. One minute she is sweating but as the shower comes down gently on her, she is beginning to shiver with cold. I am holding her with one hand and scrubbing her with the other. I am soaked. She is my sister for better or for worse but I did not expect it to come this far! My stomach is churning with fear. I take the towel and gently dry her. At that point, she murmurs something. Her teeth are rattling as she shivers more. I hold her by the shoulders and lead her back to her bed.

As they were stepping out of the shower, Baby knew in her soul that she had given her the last shower Guy would ever take in this life. Baby would never see her again.

And she never did.

When Baby brought Guy back to her bed, she reached for her chart. There was nothing other than her name. Even though Baby guessed what her sister was suffering from, she was afraid of asking in case the staff confirmed it to her. She noticed the staff exchanging knowing glances!

There was no time to ran to, sit, share or to process the hospital big event.

After that visit, they travelled to the next town to book the night train. She could not let herself feel, she had to keep going. She was the stronger one and she told herself strong people could not afford to feel, they had to keep going. Baby had been too shocked to feel the biting hunger. It was like she was driven. Her body followed her mind. She was a planner. One thought gave way to a chain of others, none of which concerned food – only life!

Her brothers were shocked beyond words and deeds but she had to have the composure to keep going. She was an organizer and this was not the time to give in to defeat and hopelessness. What needed to be done had to be done. This day was a far cry from life growing up when Baby was the youngest and weakest when she said and did what she was told to do by her older siblings.

On the journey back, Baby was too tired to sleep and her mother was too worried to sleep. It was like Mellie still relived her escaping from her husband. Mellie was scared stiff for her dying daughter and for her children. Everyone was a prime suspect as she watched for anyone who might be one of Fredrick's spies, not knowing that Fredrick and the other children had enough to worry about. Baby had also to keep watch in case her mother began another episode. It was a stressful night. The train journey took ten long hours. They would then get off, three-quarters of the way through the journey and wait until morning to catch a minibus to their home.

I am holding my mother's hand as we cross the road from the train. She is even worried about walking about with me. She keeps asking me where her children are. I am upset with her. Does she not realize I am one of her children? A tear drops! I have a bag on my back and I am stressed. I am afraid of other people hearing her talking (nonsense). In reality, I am not ready to focus on anything at this moment! I am ashamed of her talking and talking. It is as though I have been pulled into some dark hidden place taking away all that has happened in the last two days. I go into the ticket station where we find out when the bus will leave. I must bring her as I cannot even leave her on the seat alone. She is scared and thinks everyone is out to harm her. She wants to keep walking to go and look for her children. Therefore, I fear she may get lost.

I am sad, very, very sad indeed. But I am in this alone. I am paying for our tickets as she talks on and on. Shortly we go and wait in the lounge. I am trying to silence her so that others do not hear what she is saying but she is too saturated with stress to be quiet. Thoughts of how strong, capable and confident she was just a few months ago fill my mind and I get more frustrated. Am I losing my mother too? Is she dying now that her mind is gone? Is this it now? What has happened to her? I do not know what to do.

Will she ever again hear me, know what I am saying and most of all know me? She left me when I was very young and when she came back, I could not recognize her. Is this a reverse of that experience? I feel very lost and alone. Being with her and not being able to communicate is very sad indeed. These pangs of pain pierce my heart.

When Baby and her mother eventually got into the bus, they sat with a thud. They were deadbeat. Baby felt very embarrassed of her mother who kept talking. She had spent her years in the limelight and was very popular and Baby was afraid they would meet someone who had known her and ask what had happened to her brain.

Thankfully and miraculously, they did not meet anyone.

They arrived in their nearby town at around eleven o'clock the following morning. This had been the last day of the three days' off. She had planned to leave her mother at home and head immediately to her work. But her mother was quite unwell.

The dilemma was having to choose between her mother and the life call she was choosing.

So, Baby thought for a moment. Instead of going home directly, Baby and Mellie made their way to Mellie's friend's house. Her name was Jackie and she had known Mellie for many years. Jackie was a nun and they had met at church. This was years before Baby even thought of becoming a nun herself. Like Baby, Jackie was a Kenyan nun. She ran a dispensary as a nurse and she had a special love for the ill and the elderly. She was instantly moved to action the moment she saw Mellie.

Knowing Baby's involvement with the nuns, Jackie turned to her after taking care of Mellie. "Baby, we have to call your accompaniment and tell her that you cannot go back yet. Your mother needs medical attention. She has not slept for a very long time and she needs a good rest."

"I know she needs rest. I knew something is amiss and that is why I brought her with me," said Baby. Baby was so grateful for the friend she had in this woman who was able to come and step into her shoes and help out when she so badly needed it. Baby never forgot this act of kindness this woman showed when she felt weakest and most in need. Truly as the adage goes, a friend in need is a friend indeed. The friend prescribed some drugs which Baby went and bought from a chemist. Her mother slept for several days and nights, the beginning of her journey of recovery.

After they had called the sister, they drew a plan of action. As soon as they had eaten, they took Mellie to the clinic. The doctor discovered that Mellie had extremely high blood pressure and needed complete bed rest. Her mind was under siege from stress and the only way to know if it was curable was for Mellie to do nothing.

While this was occurring, Baby's friend told her about what happened to her home while Mellie was away. She did not pretend to be in the dark about it for Baby would have learned soon enough. After the visit to the doctor, Baby asked her to drive them to what had been their home!

While Mellie lay in the hospital, cared for by the kind nurses, Baby and her friend left for her old home. When they got there, they found the whole compound fenced up. They could not make out where the gate had been. It was the first time Baby had seen it since she left those months ago. The site left her mouth agape. This was another blow. Mellie had no home and a daughter slowly dying at the Kenyan coast. Baby didn't know what to do. Her mother was stressed enough.

Where were the rest of their family? Baby could not find anyone to ask and she couldn't go off in search. Her mother's health was a more important and urgent matter to attend to.

For the next week, Mellie was too drowsy to eat. She had needed more sleep than food. She was able to sleep only when she felt safe enough. This place provided the security she needed; a friend she knew and trusted.

By the end of the week, Baby sent a telegram to all her siblings whose whereabouts she knew, including the ones she had left at the coast. "Please come home urgently. Mother very ill, Baby," it read.

When they had come, she was free to go and attend to her own matters. She left Mellie in the safe hands of her elder brother Mulili who would ensure her medication and safety.

It was as if Baby's elder siblings were from a different family. The older barely knew the younger. It took some energy to gel with them. Mulili was one of those siblings. He had left the house long before Baby completed schooling. He kept to himself and hardly ever shared what he had gone through with the younger ones. He had suffered much and sometimes Baby wished he could be more of a loving brother to her. Left together she did not know what to share with him. It was a difficult situation to be in and she still hoped they would be able to form some relationship. Maybe when she was grown, he could then see her and value her as his sister!

At times she wondered how Mulili actually dealt with the difficulties faced by his family and how he negotiated the suffering and pain in his life. How difficult it must have been for him as the first boy in his family to persevere and see his family go through all they had been through. She wished they could have a forum for her brother to share even a little of what life had been for him growing up!

It occurred to Baby that Mulili had lost to death the sister he followed and his younger brother. She wondered how it was for him to cope with these deaths. Oh! Her heart went out to him. At such times her heart would soften enough to understand him.

Whatever hope Baby had for reconciliation between her and her brother would have to wait. She had to go back to formation. But when she did she kept all that she had heard and seen in her heart. She did not feel free to share with those she lived with.

Whenever they asked what had been wrong with her sister in the hospital she said she had malaria. Malaria was a safe disease to talk freely about. She did not want to talk about her sister's illness. It was loaded with shame and she did not want to give them that opportunity so easily. She was afraid people would judge her sister and it was not their place to do that.

Before a month was over after Baby returned to the nuns, one of her brothers called in on her. The phone had rung that evening and for some reason, Baby's heart skipped a beat. She went all ears as she listened to whoever had received the landline telephone. The phone was placed on an old stool at the furthest end of the corridor. The receiver's steps moved closer and closer towards the chapel where Baby sat fidgeting though her eyes were half-closed. Tap! Tap! Tap! She touched on her shoulder and whispered to Baby's ear. 'Baby, you are needed on the phone.

When Baby answered it the voice on the other end of the line asked, "How are you?" It was Mato.

Baby's heart was pounding hard. "Ok, what about you?" she replied.

"We have some bad news," Mato said.

"She is dead, is she not?" Baby interrupted.

"Yes" her brother answered after some dead silence.

Even though she had known and expected her sister's death she still mourned and mourned. She spent sleepless nights. She prayed for the repose of her soul. Her companions were very kind and mindful of her. She could not attend the funeral for it was too far away, and it would be too painful. The memories of Guy were very conflicting and truth be told there was a lot of hate. But it was still her sister and Baby found herself grieving deeply. Memories of how she had treated her and they had missed the opportunity to reconcile! Baby needed to hear her sorry and let her rest in peace. Now she had to engage with this journey even as she was on the other side of life.

Despite the fact that the family was quite scattered, Baby always took the role of organizing everyone else to support her sister's children. There were two children still with Mellie and Fredrick and they had to ensure that they were educated and taken care of. This was a difficult task when members read from different scripts. The responsibility for the children had to be shouldered immediately. Children belong to the family but Mellie had to carry the load!

Reflection Time: the impact of HIV/AIDS

Resources have been diminished by the effects of this disease so that even the living are left to eke for a livelihood. One good thing for sure is the fact that medication has become free and easily available. Therefore, those who can go against the grain of stigma can avail of the medication and are able to prolong their lives. Medication has ensured people live positively with HIV.

However, suffering in silence still remains a big blow for those affected and infected. Some people suffer in silence because they think they are the only family in the world going through this struggle. The truth is more people than we dare to think are saying the same. So, courage!

As you read this chapter, could you be suffering in silence about something? Perhaps you are afraid to tell someone you are HIV positive or someone you love is HIV positive. Or perhaps it is something else.

It is painful to watch families do what they know best when they are face to face with seemingly deadly diseases. Be around people who care enough to listen and who can help make the burden lighter. It starts by looking for someone who understands and does not judge or does not show you when they do!

What happens to the people who opt to go silent on HIV?

I have seen parents punished; children stressed up and suffering. Everyone stretched beyond their ability all because the affected or infected cannot find a way to engage with what each one is going through.

Where to begin:

Find a forum even outside of your particular setting and share how being infected or what having an infected family member does to you.

Actually, someone may understand what you are suffering right now. Someone in the world and around you and waits to listen to you.

There is healing in connecting with someone, even with one person.

Please remember that:

You did not die; you are here as you read this.

Can you take a few minutes and look back?

How far has the Lord brought you and your family?

Are there times you felt like it was definitely over only for life to shoot again in places you only saw death? SO,

What are you committing yourself to do about the situation you are facing now?

~CHAPTER EIGHTEEN~
SADNESS

If you have had a family member with a prolonged illness in the family, how have you coped with it? Some members keep off and leave a few or one member to carry the burden of caring for a sick sibling or parent on their own.

Have you fulfilled your responsibility as a son, daughter, parent or otherwise or have you evaded and 'left others to do it solely?

Some patients have died unnecessarily just because the rest of the family was not aware of what intervention needed to be got on time.

When eventually death does happen, how do those who are left cope? Sometimes death is difficult to face and families have found themselves blaming other forces.

The next year Baby did not go home. She dove into her work and her life with the nuns, trying not to think of all that had happened. But it didn't work. Her worry grew and as it grew, she became as thin as a needle. She worried about her family all the time. She felt very helpless and did not know what to do except pray for them, which she did fervently.

The next Christmas, to ease her worry, she visited her brothers at the coast, staying with Loki. He was now married to Mama Lexi and the two loved each other greatly. When Loki married her, she already had a child named Twist. Loki was working and all three members of the family were very good to each other. They had moved to a three bedroomed house and they were happy. Loki even promised to visit Baby when she went back and this excited Baby greatly. It was unheard of, a visit from her brother who never visited anyone! A brother who only came home once a decade!

There was only one problem. Sometime before, perhaps in an attempt to bond with his father, Loki had asked their father to bless alcohol on him. This was a ritual between the younger generation and the old wherein the elder generation would bless the young with the traditional brew. It was implied that the elder was welcoming the young into their company, indicating their belief that the young could handle drink responsibly. Loki knew that alcohol negatively affected him but he believed that if his father offered the drink this way it would fix him and grant him the control over it that he had lost.

Although he knew his father could not manage drink, he needed the assurance and permission from him to continue drinking. It didn't work. He would receive all his salary and sit in a bar for several days until he had spent the last penny. He bought himself a mega beer mug so he did not have to waste too much time waiting for the small glasses to get refilled. The mug held the equivalent of three beers. Baby had all these stories in the back of her mind. She had every reason to worry. Most of her family believed that he was under a certain spell when it came to drinking. She needed them to convince her how it worked but none of them could. She worked with the facts she had. This was a very difficult truth for her to face. Alcoholism was not talked about. It was assumed to be a spell or curse put upon someone by another. But it wasn't. Loki was an alcoholic! And he like Fredrick had become infected with this disease!

Baby wondered what could have been done to save him. What kind of healing did he need and who would offer it to him? She did not know why but it bothered her to see him this drunk. Looking back, she now realizes how her brother had been lonely and for many years had not kept in touch with anyone. Could this have led him to drink? Many members of this family were attracted to drink to a fault. Older and younger members it seemed needed to approach alcohol with caution! Or wisely not at all!

Three years later Loki and Mama Lexi had a baby boy. His name was Lexi. This brought more love to Loki's life. Lexi began to tame him. He gave Loki something to fight for that was stronger than any urge to drink. Loki treated his son like a king and loved him dearly. One would be hard-pressed to find a man who loved his son and family more. It looked like he was gifting Lexi what he himself found scarce because of his absent father.

It did not happen immediately but Loki's family kept their promise and went to visit Baby. It was the best thing that ever happened to her. She treasured this visit. That year Baby sat for her examination in college, passing with flying colors. She was to be a primary school teacher. Her studies had paid off and now she would work with the nuns as a teacher. Loki was the only one from her family who sent her a card. And, what's more, he had enclosed some money on it! It was a good amount of money and it was not the amount that mattered. It was that he sent it. She read the card over and over again and kept it safe where she kept her greatest treasures.

That Christmas and the next one, Baby went to visit her brother. They were now best of friends and the visits had provided space and time to get to know each other. Baby came to know her brother better than any other sibling she had. She had a lovely time and as she left, he asked her to ask their mother for her rosary beads. Baby did not ask him why he wanted this particular rosary. It was a known but an unsaid truth that their mother was a very prayerful woman and that she got her prayers answered. Their mother was only the more delighted that her son had a desire for prayer. She responded willingly though none of Baby's family except her knew it, Loki had been unwell for several years. He had had 'malaria!' The next Christmas, when Baby visited her brother, he was very ill. He was the breadwinner for his family as his wife was a housewife. He was ill but had to go to work so he paid a fellow to carry him on his bicycle. Seeing this, Baby was in tears. He went to work and ensured his family had enough to live on. When he came back home, he lay in bed unable to move. He had earned enough to push his family on for another month. He even insisted on Baby taking some money for her travels. He got offended when she declined, so eventually, she took it. She felt that her brother was generous to a fault.

At the time, no medicine could cure or even reduce the pain caused by the complicated diseases as a result of HIV/AIDS. Whatever medicine there was could only be afforded by the very cream of society.

When Baby left them that Christmas, she knew somewhere within her that she would never see him again. As she went back, he asked her to ask their mother to pray for him.

She cried for the whole journey home.

At the time there had been a visiting priest in town who was claimed to pray for people and heal all kinds of illnesses, including HIV. News about his healing gift spread in the town like wildfire as every other person talked about him and what miraculous healing they had witnessed and experienced. Baby had never seen this guy. Sure, she had nothing to lose so she decided to give this new healer a try. She had been praying directly to God to work a healing miracle to her brother. She still knew this was a hard bargain given his status, but she was given to really engaging in serious prayer for him. She prayed and prayed and kept ringing to find out how he was doing. She believed that God would answer her prayers. With time, her belief in the healing of her brother was so strong that she actually believed he was getting better.

Yeah, you have moved from the puff,
I don't deny that it's been tough,

The Change You Want is Within You

The road rough,
As you've borne the cough

This is however different
Should I say you've been patient?
I remember the days of ancient
And every act was coherent.

Loki your life
It hasn't been without rife
All through with your wife
Whom you loved more than your own life

You've taught me how to treasure
I keep this with lots of pleasure
Living for those we love like you is leisure
You've given freely and without pressure

You've lived through experience
Not without galore patience
God has shown and all can see the essence
God is showing you God's presence

I pray ceaselessly every time
That at God's own time
All your dreams may rhyme
Then all bells will chime.

Baby had been postponing calling the healing priest due to her doubts and fears but one Saturday morning Baby woke up with the strange urge that it was time. Throughout that day she looked for his contact, but it was only until that evening that she found his number and reached out to him. She took a deep breath, dialed his number with her index finger (It was the kind of phone where you put your finger on each digit at a time) and waited nervously. It was that kind of a call one needed to make and yet did not want it picked. She half expected the line would ring out before it got picked up. She was about to hang up when he picked up the phone. Her mouth momentarily went dry as she tried to remember the words she had rehearsed so many times before. He eventually said something to the effect of "Hello, can I help you?" "Yes," She said, "mmm my name is Baby, I am calling on behalf of my ailing brother ..." "Loki" he completed.

Baby's mind went blank. Was she imagining things? No, she knew what she had heard very well. She did not know this guy on the phone and yet he knew her brother's name? She did not hear what else the man of God said. She hung up and stared at the handset for a very long time as the words rang through her mind. If he knew her brother's name would he also confirm her fears? Would he say there was no hope for her brother? Baby knew Loki was close to death. It was obvious. But how did this man know? Baby was too afraid, too discouraged.

Her prayer, she reckoned, was the only option left. And this prayer seemed to make her brother worse day by day! Where was the God who used to respond to desperate prayers? To her prayers. Where was the God who they said could save?

It was during this intense prayer time that her brother Loki passed on. She received the call five months after she had visited him. It was devastating and one of the most painful losses she had ever gone through in her life. Words fell short when it came to the grief she experienced. It seemed to fill. The whole of her body. It was as though she had died with him. Even though she had known in her head this would come, it was a hard truth! She had somehow thought that God would change and let her dear brother live.

I visit you Loki and see you lying
I feel as though I'm the one dying
I'm so touched by your calm
I leave the room with that calm

What more evidence
Than that of God's presence
Dying and yet fully alive
Drained and brave

After learning of her brother's death, Baby's rage at God grew. How could God allow this? How could he do this despite all the prayer and the hoping?

In all the anger and madness, occasionally Baby's mind flitted to Loki's son. He was barely three, too young to understand death but old enough to understand that his father was no longer there. In his anger and grief, he turned against his mother and started blaming her for taking his daddy away to the hospital. "I want my daddy. I want my daddy. Why did you take him to the hospital?" the boy told his mother.

Oh! I do not know why it has taken so much of my energy to grief for you brother. I do not even know why I have taken Lexi's feelings to be like my own. I am scared of your death.

Why did you die? Are you such a coward? You could not hang in there till a drug was found and yet I kept praying to God to keep you. Of course, you still chose to die. You are such a coward! You know you were such a nice brother. I will always thank God that I got to know you and love you brother. Thank you for all the good you did. Thank you too for showing me how to be for others. I will always miss you, my big brother. Baby wondered how worse life could get. What this life had brought her face to face in ten years was a life span!

Reflection Time: Coping with loss

How can we creatively involve children when the loss of a loved one happens?

Have you ever found yourself telling someone experiencing loss to stop crying ... that it will affect the children or other women?

What if you allowed yourself to work through loss as best as you know?

Culturally people thump their feet, shake, dance, sing, tell positive stories about the departed, yell holding their heads etc. It is common knowledge that grief affects us even after many years. How has death affected you?

~CHAPTER NINETEEN~
WHERE IS GOD?

Children are often forgotten after death happens and this could cause trouble later in life for the kids. It is like everyone thinks children are too young to think or be affected by the death. It is important that orphaned children are supported in grief for them to be helped to talk about and get healing.

Her own sadness made Baby madder with God. Loki had died.

How could God allow her brother to die? Why him? After all the prayer that everyone had whispered. She had only asked for his healing. But he was not healed the way she had expected and by now Baby had experienced two deaths of her siblings. It was too much to bear. Why God? Why? The more she asked the question the more she cried!

Lord my well is running dry
My being is in a sigh
I am watching as life passes by
Like all, I love decide to die
I wish I had known
All the time you had won
For whom are you healer I wonder
And your ways to ponder

What prayer do you ever answer?
Healing would have been some peace enhancer
For he lived and served
We would have thought this he deserved

He suffered many a day
As on his bed, he lay

His family was number one
As he lived each day but for the son.

Your life was an example
Yes, you've gone but left behind a sample
I remember you with great gratitude
I thank God for your attitude

I know I don't say enough
My heart is pain-soaked and this is tough
Jesus for sure you made a fool of me
I've ever thought I had a faithful friend in thee

I am disappointed
My heart is disjointed
I will miss Loki for I loved him,
Pain is an abyss, my life dim

You were to me a real big brother
With time I will recover
Forget you, I will never
God knows when, however.

Baby went back to her family home during the time they were preparing to bury her brother. She tried to talk to her mother as a method of healing but Mellie was too shocked to talk. This was the second time Baby had seen her mom in grief, though when her sister had died they did not meet much. When there was grief it was not talked about. Death was the white elephant that all avoided discussing. When sad, Mellie withdrew into herself and so did all her children, including Baby, most of the time.

But this time was different. It was like one had to have a very big intervention to break the loud silence. Only, it didn't exactly happen that way. It was a small intervention, the first steps to healing. It began and ended with a simple question that Baby asked her mother one day when they were both sitting silently across from each other. "When is it harder for a mother, when she has lost an adult child or an infant?"

After a long pause, Mellie said, "All children are the same and one grieves for a child regardless of age."

That was it for some time. But it was the beginning. At another time, Baby said how she missed her brother Loki and how he had been there for all of them in the family.

It was a surprise when her mother responded, "You know when certain teeth break, and food will remain in the pot uneaten."

That was all that was said between the two of them.

They held the sad funeral two days after her mother told her that. In Mellie's culture and therefore in Loki's, funerals were not rushed. It took time to organize and prepare properly. This funeral, like all, was very sad indeed. Loki had two sons; Twist was a teenager and Lexi barely three years old. As they brought the body of their father home for burial Lexi asked 'Mami ninini iko kwa hiyo sanduku?' (Mummy! What is in that casket?) Mama Lexi had told him they were going to collect a 'load' from the hospital. Nobody had the heart to tell him what was really in the box. If only he would be less interested in the coffin.

The two boys kept together and the extended family did not know how to help them go through this grief. Everyone seemed too overwhelmed to think of them. Each of the family members were completely immersed in their own loss and nobody, not even their mother, knew what to do.

Lexi never stopped blaming his mother for taking his dear father to hospital. As his father's body was being lowered, he cried and cried. Then later he asked his mother where his dad had gone. She told him that he had gone to God. "Is that the God who took my dad?" he asked as he pointed at a crucifix on the wall.

"Yes," his mother answered. "I want to go where dad is," his mouth whispering what his heart moaned quietly.

Baby had known that Mama Lexi was ill all along but she never imagined that she would die so soon. After the funeral, Mama Lexi returned to the coast and it was quiet for five months. They all thought that she would go on with life as usual. Then they got the news that she was admitted to the hospital. Two weeks later she died. She had kept it quiet and nobody knew. As well as mourning her husband, she also had to face the reality of her failing health.

Lexi's heart was broken again and this time it was beyond repair. He was never the same. He closed into himself, disappeared into an unreachable place only he knew. This little boy seemed to mirror Baby, her shadow self. It was like she was grieving for both herself and him. Watching him so grieved made Baby sad indeed.

He withdrew so inwardly that no one could reach him, he did not relate much and gradually lost interest in life. He just sucked his thumb and sat on his own. Baby was lost for words. She wanted to work on herself and him as well. She didn't want to be like Lexi.

Years later, after finishing primary school and enrolling in an all boy's seminary school, Lexi went to live with his uncle. One day, around eight o'clock in the evening, three men came to visit his uncle's house. Nobody knew the details but Lexi, his uncle and his aunt were taken; something to do with a grudge against the uncle. They were found a few days later, slashed to death by machetes.

Lexi's dreams, his youth and promising life was violently taken from him at the age of seventeen. He went to join his dear parents!

And some heart-rending wounds take forever to heal! The sad near closure of a family!

But this was not until many years in the future. At the time, another grievance took Baby's mind. It took Baby years to grieve for the loss of her brother. And in those years, a year before Lexi got admitted to the seminary school, Fredrick died.

It was strange really. Fredrick had tormented everyone and though none would allow themselves to admit it, his death was always pictured as a relief. But now, fourth in the succession of deaths within the family, it felt more painful than ever. Instead of relief, it was a reminder of the others who had died. It was as though death had come to plague them.

A man of Fredrick's age deserved – though perhaps Fredrick did not – a funeral attended by all family unless there was an extremely grave reason as to why one could not attend. Even though he had often ridiculed the church, Fredrick had been an elder in the church during his later years and the church took over the proceedings to give him a fitting send-off. There was a requiem mass at the local church followed by a burial at his home.

By the time Fredrick died, some of the family had attained a sense of equilibrium. Some of the older children had met him and Mellie and had talked about the effects of their choices earlier in their marriage. Grievances were vented and apologies were made. While forgiveness was given and peace was achieved, a certain level of acceptance was established and the children had accepted responsibility for caring for their ageing parents. Therefore, before Fredrick died, he had gained some level of parental respect and pride in his children.

Even Guest showed up to the funeral. Perhaps she would have wished to miss it, but as a child of the Kamba culture, she could not. In the last days of life, forgiveness was meant to be achieved so that when the children buried their parents, the dead could rest in peace. A good relationship with a parent ensured blessings in one's life.

How Fredrick rested, nobody would ever know.

Fredrick rested forgiven!

Reflection Time: Children and Death

How can you support children to cope with loss?

If this is a difficulty for you can you ask someone else to help them out?

When people have lost dear ones and everyone else thinks they are doing well it would be significant to check regularly how they are doing and offer them a shoulder.

When people suffer loss and a great one like the loss of a dear husband, companion or child, how often do you reach out to them to see how they are coping after the funeral?

How can you support family, friends or neighbors even after they have buried their loved one?

As our loved ones die, how does it influence us to use our time fully by giving our best while being aware we too can follow any time?

If I wasted my time in the past, how can I contribute to the world devotedly to be of help to others around me so that when my time is up I will have given all I had to?

~CHAPTER TWENTY~ THE CHANGE BABY WANTS IS WITHIN

What are the 'skeletons' in your family?

(These are in the form of family secrets we would rather not touch, what may be amazing is that couples carry similar family secrets and these could be what attracts them to each other. It is of paramount importance to understand our family secrets other than falling into patterns unaware!) Many times, these affect the living in the family system negatively.

It was another several years before Baby could do anything other than survive emotionally. She worked and lived her life as normal. But she felt dead inside, numb to life as she had been forced to become numb to death.

After her examination, Baby went to work as a primary school teacher. She was meant to start directly after her examinations, working at the local school run by the nuns, but the series of deaths postponed her start. It was not until after a great deal of courage that she began her teaching career.

When she did, she found work harder than she had ever imagined. The teaching was easy and Baby had a knack for it. But many of the children Baby taught were from the slums. They had little and it wasn't uncommon to hear of a father or mother dying in the night. The children would still come to school! Here, too, death seemed to plague Baby.

The first day of class, Baby walked in and saw three of the students with small black marks on their uniform. "What is this?" Baby asked, trying to strike the chimeric balance between being strict and being kind.

The three students looked at the ground for a moment. Then one of them whispered, "There was a fire last night. We threw our extra clothes away but it burnt through." Baby paused. What did this child mean by 'extra clothes'? She nodded as she deeply listened. "Are you ok?"

The students nodded.

Over the course of the day, Baby noticed more and more scars on the arms and legs of the students. She saw the burn marks from the fires that frequently swept through the slums. During lunch, she asked her fellow teacher why the children wore 'extra clothes'.

"It is so if they catch fire, there will still be clothes to wear to school."

Baby didn't ask anymore. She was afraid to know more, afraid to ask if the teacher was using '*they*' to refer to the clothes or the students.

Life as a teacher seemed no less overwhelming than life before but at least Baby understood. Deep down Baby understood the struggles of these children for they were not far removed from the struggles she had faced.

Baby was full. Full of her long-life experiences, to the brim!

When I eventually decide to go for counselling, I have come to a space in myself where I need things to change as I am not contented with the way my life is. I feel like there is some potential I have not attained like things could be better but I wonder how. I feel life is meaningless. I now realize that I am just going through life without awareness. I am either in the past or in the future a future which I do not see myself experiencing.

I cannot see myself reaching forty - I already wish to die before then. I am preoccupied with death. Does this send chills down your spine? If not I am sharing that I am depressed. I am more comfortable alone and life is a chore. I am so smart that even people do not realize I am suffering as much as I am because I avoid them. I cry a lot at night and by morning I am up and doing as if nothing happened. I have got allergies and I have phototropic glasses that I wear all the time to make it difficult to look into my eyes as this would betray me. I am in my world. I am 'screaming' inside.

Eventually Baby began to trust herself more and make a few friends. She knew a good friend when she met one and a few years after the plague of deaths, she became friendly with a woman named Anna who had lived with her as a lodger for some time. Anna was tall and full of confidence. She was respectful and purposefully engaged when talking to someone. She was well-grounded and loving and caring. This was a friendship Baby doubted would last at all but she might as well see. She had had friends before and they did not stay.

It would be some time before Baby looked back on her friendship with Anna, sometime before she realized its significance. The friendship, Baby would realize in later years of her life, lasted longer than she could imagine and had a great influence on her life. Anna's friendship was instrumental to Baby's journey as it was beginning to develop in relation to how she wanted to live her remaining life. She wanted to work on what life has been and engage with her journey of freeing herself and living consciously

I tread carefully
I study, weigh and know
At times it's done dreadfully
Other times I just don't trust the inferno.

Though slow, the base is love
This sets my heart free
Bringing peace and joy above
The mind, heart and conscience agree

And it feels like a coup
What is in those eyes?
And all is laid open, I've no clue

There is warmth in what was ice

Take the phone to say hello
If you're true, they'll know your state
Even the pauses bellow
Then you begin to believe at last you are great.

A friend is a gift
A friend's a treasure
I allow to rise and drift
A friend helps reduce life's pressure.

Baby was experiencing an expansion of her heart she never had before. She was stretching herself to talk about her experiences, about her life. In the past, she would only say very little and that was it. But now it seemed she could share and be open with this friend. It was hard at times and she often found herself becoming closed off. But she also felt strong enough to try, strong enough to fight her closed and withdrawn self.

She began to learn that, for relationships to work, communication was vital. It was a new experience, a new revelation for her. The entirety of her life had been telling her the opposite. To survive you had to build a shell, you had to do nothing but continue, push forward and ignore the pain and suffering.

But now she was promising to talk about what she experienced in order to change the pattern of her life and of her short-lived relationships. These experiences helped her get in touch with her strengths and weaknesses. She finally found the strength to continue to struggle not to get through life but to get to know life as it unfolded. Until then she had thought that everyone around her needed to change so that she would be at peace – her father, mother, siblings and others. She now keenly observed how all that she wanted to be changed in others was also found in her. This was very humbling.

Baby was conscious now and as her consciousness grew, she realized that she had to work through her not-so-pleasant experiences in her life from her childhood. Her family history held a lot of information which would help her to appreciate all the aspects of her personality. She was willing to open up her family's box of skeletons – more like a warehouse of skeletons. She could pick and focus on one at a time. Only then could she continue.

Reflection Time: Taking risks

Are we condemned to our past?

Can we permit ourselves to be the message we came here to bring and be the people God created us to be?

What risks do you need to take at this moment of your life? Name 5 areas of your life you need to take a risk in.

What do you need to learn to be the best version of yourself?

~CHAPTER TWENTY-ONE~
THE FEAR OF DEATH

Inner work takes a lot of energy, time and commitment.

How much are you willing to sacrifice to heal and become the best of who you can be?

Baby loved drawing, reading and writing. This was one way she could freely express herself when her tongue was tied. She expressed herself through other means too, like painting and molding clay. Her creative work was very insightful into her deeper journey of self-exploration. When she drew she put out her feelings and was able to cope better with whatever situation she was in, being able to visually experience whatever was within her heart. It was a solution during the hours of therapy where she sat in involuntary silence, unable to put her deep-seated pain and sadness into words.

Along with therapy, which was recommended, Baby was required to be accompanied by a spiritual director. This suited Baby, for she was a spiritual person and a part of her always wanted a spiritual mentor who could guide her to be the best she could be. This director was a big man with a deep voice which Baby found soothing and grounding to listen to. But something was missing. She could still not fully open up.

Baby knew fairly early on in her adult life that she needed therapy. Everybody needed therapy. But she didn't end up deciding until some years after joining the nuns and being encouraged to take the step. Her therapist was a calm and composed woman who reminded her of the stereotypical therapists; peaceful. Her office was carpeted and gave the feeling of home. The walls were beautifully painted with bright colors and the room was big enough to hold three comfortable sofas. There was always a lit candle which gave off a nice scent as it burnt. As well as the sofas, there were big, cozy, colorful cushions that one could sit on if they didn't want the sofa. Working materials like crayons, papers, clay and more either lay atop the desks or within the drawers, always in their allocated spots. A three-foot-tall Dragon Tree sat in the corner.

Through these relationships, she had done a lot of downloading, a lot of taking in the advice and recommendations of her mentors. But still, other skills were greatly needed to get her to deeper healing. She was forever grateful to them for witnessing the beginning of her long journey and the opening of her well-locked inner door. But it was just the beginning.

She was a shy person, Baby. No one else in her family was shy. Many of her family were reserved but that was not the same. She was very soft-spoken and she hated it when anyone asked her to speak louder. She got very angry when she felt unheard. She was evidently different in personality from the rest of her family. It felt as though her destiny was very unique and she wanted to find out as much as she could about herself. It was this fascination and deeper searching that led her to another phase. It was not until Baby did a workshop entitled '*Be the Change you Want to See in the World*' that life began to take a turn.

The workshop focused on the participant not only as the instrument of change but also the subject of change. So often Baby had heard that she needed to change the world around her, so often had she heard it was about looking outward. But here she was told to look inward, to dig deep into her values and beliefs. She needed to look inside to heal what prevented her living her life to the fullest.

This was the chance, the opportunity to jump into the healing pool. Time never felt any fitter and riper. The workshop consisted of a good bit of bodywork. It seemed to touch on something Baby could buy into. The work with the body fascinated her. She was carrying the stress and life story in her body; like a continuously heavy load, she had to push up a slippery hill.

Unlike most one-off workshops, this was held three times during the year. It was designed to push the participants to engage with themselves and to hold them accountable throughout this engagement. Before the year was out Baby could see improvement. She was off on her healing journey, gaining understanding. Could Baby be depressed? No way! She didn't even want to entertain the thought! There were times she found it difficult to get in touch with what she felt. Once in a while words may touch only the tip of what was the deep sea.

I feel very low and feel like I am dying slowly. I find it difficult to cope with everything. I feel tired. I feel stressed and stretched. I feel overworked and unproductive. Dead. I want to disappear, to just give up work. Work does not give me satisfaction. I feel like I am dying slowly. I am struggling and using every ounce of energy to survive.

For a while after this conference, Baby's eyes began to become dead and she found herself in such a faraway place that no one could reach her. The brighter side of her life had disappeared within her into an unknown place. She had taken to wearing sunglasses so that no one could see through the windows of her soul. She was in a daze. She didn't want anyone to look into her eyes lest they see how depressed she was. But only two persons seemed to know and understand what Baby was going through, her workshop director and her friend. Her best friend who had seen the sadness in her eyes said to her once; "Baby, I am glad you have taken this courageous step. I envy your courage. I will be here to support you through every step of the way."

She had taken to avoiding people. Her voice was slowly disappearing into the bottomless pit within her. Whenever she talked, she felt like she had to move the whole world to get to her voice.

Some wisdom inside her knew very clearly that something had to be done urgently. Those around her did not think so! She was a young sister why would she need to. By now Baby, (who was in her late twenties), thought it would be a bonus to live up to forty! Every minute was an effort to exist. Her spiritual director supported her through the journey to negotiate with the right people to allow for help.

One day her best friend met her at the airport and expressed her concern about how withdrawn Baby looked. Baby did not think what she felt showed on the outside. She did not engage much and was just there dragging her body along as it had to keep going. She felt like she wanted to go to a faraway place. She woke up one morning at dawn and started walking away .... Her friend woke up in time to see her and follow her up. She got her back! This scared her friend! They did not know what was happening.

Her friend simply smiled and handed her a notebook. "Do not use it unless you really want to. I just thought it might be something you would be interested in."

Baby didn't know what to say. She tucked the notebook into her possessions and carried on with the day. When she arrived home and was alone, she took it out again and opened it up. On the first page was scribbled: 'Remember I'm supporting you and cheering you on every step of the way...I pray you to begin to see and accept the amazing woman that I know you are.'

Baby began to cry. She had numbed her life to hide the pain but it all came back now. She had held strong for so many years. She had thought that she had to hold courageously. Really, this bit was true! She couldn't hold any longer. She was losing it! Whether she was breaking apart or open she did not know! What had supported her till then was wavering! She looked at the philosophies and beliefs she had adopted from childhood and saw they could no longer serve her anymore. Her voice within began to change. It had to change.

There's no point of expressing my needs as they won't be met anyway.

I need no one, I have no needs.
I am not safe and so I do not trust.
There is no one there to listen to me.
Others need me though I do not need them.
My story is not worth telling.

Or is it?

Baby began to look at how these scripts had served her over the years. She felt very scared like the ground was being pulled out from under her feet. She felt panicky and shaken. All these feelings brought a great deal of pain and shock through her system and shook her foundations. Was she able to hold on and survive the intense pain? All she knew was that she could go through pain whatever the intensity, but it had never been this much. Emotional work was proving to be like opening tins of octopus, she couldn't pull out one that was not attached to another. Wherever she turned, there was a network of emotions trying to catch her attention. She was the one everyone in her family called upon. They would never imagine their warrior would be feeling this vulnerable. Who was going to be there to hold her through this not knowing? As a friend of hers once said, 'the teachers kept coming until she grasped the lesson." How was she to expose herself to the lessons when she was so unsure anymore?

Baby was saturated with emotions and had to look for other ways to make the body release what it has held on for years. Sometimes she even contemplated death, wondering whether there was any hope in a life lived this way. She needed something. If the issue of depression was in the tissue, then some physical release was needed. Even though she needed a lot of encouragement to engage her body in her healing, she decided she would engage her body for all it was worth. She took to going for long walks into the countryside, having a weekly massage, going for weekly yoga, dancing and having daily meditation.

She had grown up in the country, running, exploring and walking for miles. She had forgotten the feeling of mobility, forgotten the desire to be at one with nature. Gradually, her once stiff body began to relax and feelings began to shift. She was more aware of her body and what happened in it when she experienced different emotions.

There was a glimpse of hope at the end of the tunnel. This gave her more energy and purpose. Inner work for Baby was a full-time job and extremely tiring. She had never experienced such pain. At times, she wished she had the option to till the soil on a farm rather than do this inner work!

Dealing with grief had been a difficult thing. Baby had many deaths in her family which she had not dealt with. She began to brace for impact, always expecting someone close to her to die. She would look at her friends and think of her family. 'How soon?' she would think. It was a difficult inward journey which cost her every ounce of energy to face each day. She chose to deal with whatever her psyche brought up. Painful and tiring though it was, she inched on as she believed she had to go through this phase to come out transformed. She engaged in what she believed she had to do for her to thrive.

Baby changed therapy.

Baby's therapist who was accompanying her on this journey saw something in Baby and began the steps towards supporting her to give Baby back to herself. She offered her all there was to offer. She stood there like a tree in support of Baby. She believed in her like only two others had ever done. She professionally awakened skills in Baby that Baby had forgotten existed in her. Baby had been so stressed that she was losing her ability to cope. Baby's therapist worked with her and was always there for her until Baby found her own feet.

"Baby, you matter," she said one day. "You are important and you have an important message to share in life. You are one hell of a powerful lady. This is your journey, take courage. I am going to stand by you. I do want to walk with you". Hearing statements like these made Baby make the baby-steps of looking at the resources she had inside and wanting more and more to discover what that scary power within her was. Her journey had started and there was no turning back, not now, never. This seemed to be the push she had always waited for, all these years; to jump in and jump in she did.

The beauty in the family
I hear I am really
Trusting, happy, lively, outgoing and free
I enjoy every moment to a large degree

At what age was my life's termination?
But for my strong - determination
When did my heart get blocked?
Opting for safety within where I'd it locked

For long I sat and went on

The Change You Want is Within You

Watched, waited as they carried on
Convinced that as I sat by the pool
That time was the only tool

When they knocked at my heart
I opened, looked and shut
Yes! For decades none was trustworthy enough
Looking up, sitting by the pool, waiting was tough

At the age, I knew I had to make a try
Prepared to jump in - then - I let others pass-by
I knew deep within I was a ceded land
To recapture the oasis, had to walk and dare the sand

I woke up, came by, looked and knew
Knew this visit to the pool was new
I looked at Him and felt I could trust
I'd been worn out, tired and my trust had rust

The pool still calm
As the angel waited for my palm
To reach through to my heavy heart
And surely gave me an upstart.

So, after all, there are people within
When into my abandoned world, I crawled in
I set out to recapture my life fully
I can live it consciously and carefully.

Even though Baby was aware of how great people said she was, she never believed it herself. She thought they said that just to make her feel good. Through her therapist's encouragement, she began to think 'why not, there may be something little somewhere.' These thoughts filled her with dread and excitement. She wanted to release that energy within her. She didn't know how to go about it. She felt like the power in her was familiar, like she once knew it. She wanted to be, to rise, to touch it in her heart but something always held her back - paralyzed her!

Reflection Time: Challenge your beliefs

Take time now and write down your own limiting beliefs.

At our core, we are made for connection with others and our limiting beliefs keep us away from others and most of all from ourselves and our mission in life.

In what way are you disconnected and how can you reconnect with the source of your life?

How do your limiting beliefs affect others and prevent you from allowing them to be as unique beings?

~CHAPTER TWENTY-TWO~
THE CHAMPION WITHIN

Death brings about a lot of fear. Ultimately it is our own death that we are afraid of. It is difficult to watch those we love as they die. This brings us closer and closer to us the reality of our inevitable extinction. Religion or spirituality makes this reality easier to grasp.

When we have parents or loved ones ailing for a long time staying present to their life and ours can be a great challenge. Some members have been so 'impatient with themselves', they have hurried the process of transition for their loved ones.

While it can be tiring and demanding of every ounce of energy and love, we can use this precious time to mend fences and to repair relationships soiled earlier on in life with our loved ones.

Staying conscious of how we accompany those in similar situations as above can be an act of Mercy.

Being mindful of what we say about people's loved ones is compassion.

Doing our inward healing journey is the call. It is about what feelings we experience and honoring that to be good companions.

Being present is a gift.

During the time that Baby was still dealing with grief, she dreamt that her mother was walking away, carrying a big black bag. Baby tried to call her mother in the dream but Mellie kept walking toward the gate without looking back. The next day Baby rang Mellie. She knew deep within her something was very wrong with her mother's health. She could not tell what, but she just knew it. Her mother's speech was so slurred on the phone that Baby could not hear what she was saying. Was her mother dying? Mellie had sent for her first-born daughter and son. The more information Baby gathered about her mother's health, the more uneasy she felt. Did her mother feel that she was dying? Baby's insides felt disconnected. She was so scared.

I feel very unsafe. I am shaking from head to toe. If my mother dies, I will die too. My life is hers and hers is mine and so I have to protect her. My heart is beating fast, my tummy is churning and I feel nauseated. My shoulders ache and my insides are hanging loose. My life is under threat –the threat of death. I wish I could shout aloud. 'Please, mother, do not die. Please do not go. Not now...do not go...who will remain with me?' I weep bitterly. I feel this threat so near me. Oh! My heart aches. The distance is killing me. Somehow I know mother will wait for me. She will hang on. I know it deep inside me. Oh! The pain is unbearable.

The moment Baby woke up from her dream she began planning to go and see her mother. She couldn't just leave as she had responsibilities, so she planned to leave in a few days. At her next therapy session, a day before she was to depart, she explained the dream. She had experienced it every night for the last three nights. Her therapist sat there for a moment. "How old is this scared child?"

Baby rested there for a moment. "I don't know. Sometimes she is a child around ten, sometimes she is only a foetus."

"Can you take this child by the hand and reassure her that her mother is safe and that someone responsible is taking care of her. Tell her that this someone is responsible and resourceful. Tell the child that she is too young to care for her mother. Tell her that it is not her responsibility to care for her mother."

Please do not say that. I am a daughter of Africa and it is within my DNA to care for my parents. I find it very difficult and saddening. What do I do? I do not want to hear those words. They scare me silly and I am afraid I will die as well.

"I will try," Baby responded, unable to explain to Sr. Norah (her European therapist) the cultural war on interdependence that was going on within her mind.

The Change You Want is Within You

Let me grow on you
My roots are not deep enough
Let me depend on you
I am fragile, let me

You are a strong rock-a cracked rock
All I ask for is to be in your cracks
Once, I was a strong rock
Sun cracked me, the strong powers

I know I'm cracked now
I'm also disintegrating,
I am weathering and integrating.
To this, I bow

Grow in my cracks and help down to weather
I need to open my lock'
After cracking, hope I can hold together
Otherwise, I won't be out of this block

Becoming me will be fine
You worry me though so small
It looks like healing is a sign
To find you my little self, I'll give my all

Mom, are you coming to your end? Can I live without you? Please my mother, hang in there till I come. I know even then I won't be ready. I want to talk to you and be there for you. I want to treasure all you have been to me and others. Just remember you are the star of my life. I am very scared and feel unsafe. My tummy churns. My eyes sting with tears and I am so sad that I cannot lift my spirit.

I want to tell you all that I have not said to you that mother you are the best mother that ever was. I want to hold you and say I love you.

Baby thought what if – just what if – it was true her mother was dying. The therapist had been helping her get in touch with her fear of death for a while now but this was different. She was so far away from her mother; how could she imagine anything other than the worst? Baby began to fear the phone. Every ring terrified her. That was how she heard about all the other deaths in the family. It felt like it was only a matter of time until Mellie's death was announced over the phone too.

I am in a safari park and as we stroll along we find this pride of lions lying in the long grass. My little niece is talking loudly and I am scared the animals will hear us. Soon after that, another pride appears in front of us. We start running and now there is only my nephew who is running ahead of me. We come to a fence and he jumps over. Being too close to him I am not fast enough to have the momentum to jump over. He gets hold of my hand to help me over. The lion is right at my rear. I think that I am dead. I just know that the lion will kill me. I feel bile-like acid moving from my toes to my head. I wake up hot like hell.

Baby decided to take the bull by the horns and face the fear head-on. She thought of what her mother had been to her, just in case Mellie had come to her end. She thought of her mother's endearing name in her mother tongue. She remembered fondly some of the commonest words that her mother used in her day-to-day life. She thought of her favorite songs her mother had taught her when she was young. *Hosanna in the Highest* immediately came to mind.

Then Baby's thoughts turned to the use of these songs in her mother's funeral. They would be used for her mother's funeral in memory of her humor and faith.

If she was to die.

When she had arranged her mother's possible funeral in her mind, she prayed, "Please God, grant my mother another ten years please. Do not allow her to die, my God".

As she prayed this prayer, Baby's neck stiffened immediately. It became so stiff she could not turn it to the left and when she tried to move it, it hurt like hell. All the yoga and all the massages didn't prevent the immediacy of the pain and stiffness, like a reflex to reflection.

The day Baby was set to leave, she called her mother. She wanted to see if anything had happened if there was any news!

"Hello," Mulili answered.

"Where is mom?!" Baby screamed. If Mulili answered the phone, then what had happened to her mother? She didn't have time to ask how he was or how he even knew of Mellie's ailing health.

"She is in hospital."

Baby froze and Mulili continued. "She is fine."

"What?"

"Her blood pressure is very high and she has been stressed and has continued to work when she shouldn't be but she is fine. She is resting in hospital but will be out soon."

This was very talkative for Mulili. He was not known for long sentences. Baby decided to push for one more.

"Why are you there though?"

"I was contacted by her neighbors when she got sick. Do not worry, Baby. Mother is fine."

Baby hung up the phone and sat back in her chair. She shivered and the tension in her neck began to dissipate. Her mother was fine. If only her heart could believe. She knew her brothers misread critical issues when it came to her parents. This was one such a one.

Her mother was fine?

Reflection Time: The fear of death ... ultimately our own.

Ask yourself if you are aware of any death issues that you may need to work through to enable you to live purposely?

How can you face your fears especially the fear of death?

What do your dreams reveal to you?

How can you spend every opportunity that you have with our elderly parents, children, community so that when death comes we have no regrets about what we could have said for them or done?

If your loved ones have already died, what do you regret not doing?

~CHAPTER TWENTY-THREE~ HONOURING

How patient are we with our growth?
How well do we know our family of origin?

Take some time to find out about your father's and mother's families.
Sometimes we carry and live with the stories of shame and guilt in our families. What are those stories you are embarrassed about your birth, mother, father and marriage realities our parents engaged with and we are here as a result? Honoring our parent's journeys is honoring ourselves.

As Baby was learning to assert herself in her relationships, she discovered she had to provide herself with the direction for her life too. She realized that it was her total responsibility to change her scripts that had fallen short of service and be for herself all she needed from others. She could only believe in her story enough to tell it. She had lived and survived till then and she had a right to be alive and thrive.

She realized that all she needed was within her. All she needed to focus on was what she had and what she could do with all she had. She imagined how life would be different if she began to live by her new script, to be fully who she was meant to be. She saw two futures, both six years ahead. She could continue with this script or get a new one. The old one showed images of loneliness. The new one:

I am enjoying my life more
My life is more meaningful
Every minute of my life counts
I am fully alive
I am more trusting in my relationships

Every year, sometimes twice a year, Baby continued attending the retreats she had begun when she became a nun. After seeing this vision of her two futures she spent a lot of time reflecting on how much more therapy she could do, how far further into her soul she could reach. After all, it had been some time and she had made a world of progress. As she thought these things she headed to the retreat center.

It was not a big retreat but it was an escape from life for a few days in a center just outside the city where someone could stop and think without the world pounding on their front door. On this retreat, she drew several pictures and portraits. On the penultimate morning of the retreat, as she was perusing through the pages to show her therapist the 'right' picture, she accidentally opened the page of a portrait she had done sometime before. It was meant to be a self-portrait but as she stared at it she recoiled in horror. The portrait she had drawn was of her deceased father. She jumped back as she saw it.

"Let's talk about that," her therapist smiled. Baby sat back in the chair. The rest of the retreat had been blurred by this image, this realization and now Baby straightened her back in her therapist's office, back in the work of the working.

"No," she said quickly, shutting her drawing book. But Baby wasn't in control here and that portrait became the topic for that session and many others thereafter. Baby was the image of her father. When people saw her in her old village even if they had never seen her before, they would ask, "Are you Fredrick's daughter?"

Over the years, Baby had slowly learned more about her father and his life before she entered the world. It was this history which took much of the therapy session. Fredrick was the first-born of his family and when his younger sibling was born his father was murdered as they had gone looking for pasture some long-distance away. Fredrick had been killed by his kin. This was never talked about as the Christian kin termed it a 'sinful death.' Fredrick's father was murdered so Fredrick's uncle could marry Fredrick's mother. It was one of the many secrets her father had kept tightly tucked away. The murderer fathered the rest of his four siblings. Fredrick had been forced to recognize the man who murdered his father as his father and recognize the man's children as his brothers and sisters.

Where did this fit in, in his newly found Christian and Catholic religion without shame?

Baby wondered if this complication in his life drove him to the brew. She guessed that there was probably a great deal of shame connected with his family. It was amazing that he did not talk about his family, but how could he? Did he want to protect his family from the complexity of his origin? If so then there was something to admire in his secrecy.

How must he have felt when he realized that he had drunk away his land and family assets as well as all the cattle? He was an African man who was expected to provide stability for his family. Did he experience guilt and shame and had he used alcohol as a coping method? He surely had tried to cope as much as he was able to in his circumstances.

She often wondered if he knew how he had impacted his family. Her heart went out to her father as she thought of what could have happened to his life, how it could have turned out. *What is happening?* She was filled with compassion for him. *He caused great misery for mother and for me. Why do I feel this way?* It was clear that life had happened to him. Maybe he had coped the best way he knew how. *No!* Yes. Even though her father's actions had impacted her negatively, *so negatively,* he had done the best he could.

Like her father, she was very hardworking, industrious, enterprising and quiet. He never wasted many words if one would do. *I do not like this game.* She was as tall as him and of chocolate complexion. *That is irrelevant.* She carried in herself his blood and had the same temperament. Baby's dad was dead and she still had a choice to 'work with him' and let him rest in peace. *No.* Or ignore him and live in misery. *I prefer that option.* The choice to live with and accept her family's past was not easy for Baby and she fought it greatly. Piece by piece, one foot at a time, she began again, for the how-many hundredth time she didn't know.

Sometimes the days are bright
Sometimes it feels so right
Just to sit in the light
Or to stand erect and upright

It has been a long race
Through the years I can trace
The healing journey which started in grace
This has picked up in pace

Won't a few months heal?
The inner journey is proving quite a deal
Short time, too short, it seems to seal
Hence for another several moons, healing I'd need to feel

For my body remembers
What my brain disremembers!
And no matter what embers!
I need out of these chambers

Baby was deeply spiritual and insightful. She found solace in God as she kept searching to know and understand herself. She knew she needed to be in touch with her inner wisdom and only God could provide that connection. She believed in a God who continually made her be her best self. She was forever grateful for all God had seen her through, what God had done for her and what God would continue to provide for her in her life. Gratitude was her commonest prayer and she believed that God was always faithful. God would not disappoint her. She believed that since God had been so generous with her she wanted to be generous when dealing with others. She always had enough for herself and others. That's partly why she burnt the midnight oil, especially in her work. She always looked out for those who were in need and those whose pain no one else saw. She always tried as much as possible to be guided by God in all she served. There was no way she was going to accept herself without accepting her roots.

It had taken her many years to accept that reality. Her parents had done the best they could. No matter what, she was grateful for them for they helped her be the best version of herself. All the flaws and all that would always be part of her as she did her life's journey of continually being conscious. Her resilience had been tried and strengthened through and for life.

Reflection Time: Growth as a process

Sometimes, these roots affect us today and we need not only to know but also to heal through prayers and conscious breaking of some negative energetic chains.

Would any father want to have such an effect on his children as happened in this chapter?

What could those reading this book and preparing to be parents or are already parents do so that the cycle of what happened to them does not happen to their children?

~CHAPTER TWENTY-FOUR~
CONCLUSION

Baby was always grateful to everyone, especially the women, who day in, day out give all they are so that others can live.

Every morning Alima is aware that the slit
Through which she sees the world could be trusted or not
Her dress is a source of pride for culture and religion.
Though others too look at her suspiciously
And above all, she's a mother.

Every morning Wanjiku wakes up
Knowing that her wealth is in her hands
The farm, the animal, the business
All her children, be a wife, a sister in law
And above all, she's a mother.

Atieno too wakes up aware of her duties
Marry and have children, be a wife for as long as she lives.
She values being one of many wives when she has a choice
She believes her husband loves her when he beats her
And above all, she's a mother.

Mrs. Kittony knows too that her fate lies with her husband
She is rated as the children since she is a woman
She, like children, cannot decide!
She is as good as the cow he owns
And above, all she's a mother.

The Change You Want is Within You

Koki prays to see the dusk her fate's uncertain
Praying she gets some casual labor to feed her children
Husband waits for the hard-earned cash
He has already sold their land for a drug.
And above all, she's a mother.

Mama Koinange's girl in the city does night shifts
She arms herself with the weapon - some rubbers
Off to Koinange Street hoping for a heavy-pocketed guy.
The deadly virus is not worth the thought
And above all, she's a mother.

Food, clothes, fees and house rent ....
Her list of needs is endless
Life is life, she is single
Into a deep abyss with limited options!
And above all, she's a mother

The barren woman cries for a child all night
She's a witch in their eyes
She could do anything even to get a stillbirth
It could earn her 'some' respect, she would be someone
Above all, she's to blame for she should be a mother.

Like a sword that is never taken to battle before it has been tried, Baby knew she has been through a great deal of a life and was grateful to God for it. It made her who she was today.

Dear younger self,

It is very nice to be able to write to you for the first time in my life. You were brought to my attention many years back. I want to spend time with you and to find out more about you. I want to love you, care for you, listen to you and hear what you want to say to me. I want to protect you, smile at you and give you what you want.

I want us to play and I will be there for you.

I am glad I have got to know you and love you when there is still time. I don't want to waste any more time but to love you with all my heart. You are the best thing that ever happened in my life. I treasure you. I want to spend a lot of time getting to know you better. All I know is that I will be there for you and I will always love you and listen to you. I will take care of you. I just want you to know that you can count on me to be there whenever you need me.

Thanks for showing up in the ways you have in the past. Thanks for directing my way. Thanks for speaking your wisdom and now I know I am because I listen to you. I know you have brought out a lot of issues but I will let you direct me in choosing what you want us to focus on.

This promise I want to make to you that I will continue to be aware of how you feel and I will stay! Even when it kills me to death, I will stay with you... together we can go through it... Thanks. I appreciate all the giants and especially my mother on whose shoulders I have stood because we all stand on the shoulders of giants.

Bye for now, Yours ...

Mellie stirred under the jacaranda outside her house. She stretched with her arms out. "Oh! God of Mercy!" It was now nearly noon and her family were up and doing. All had gone about their duties. The wrinkles she saw in the little pocket mirror as she smiled reminded her that she was eighty- three and happy. Who would have imagined that life would have turned out this way? Even though part of her life has been difficult, she could see how Our Lady walked with her. She was living the life of her dreams. It was time for the Angelus and she Hailed Mary with such delight and deep gratitude in her heart!

She has never let me down. You can see how shiny her rosary has become. She is a faithful woman.

Mellie basked in the young morning rays. She could feel the warmth between her shoulders; it was just what the doctor ordered – it was the right temperature and the right place. Gratitude filled not only her heart but her soul too and her beautiful smile was all written on her face!

When Mellie looked up she saw Baby holding this book seated under the bougainvillea tree just a few meters from her. As their eyes met they knew they had been on a long life's journey connecting their hearts in silence. They nodded at each other in an apparent Amen!

Mellie was forever grateful for carrying Baby her last born to term. She lifted the neckline of her dress to spit gently on her chest. (This was a ritual for blessing another). She accompanied it in the following words, "if you ever pass through a plain which is burning may you always find a cool tuft to step on". She spat three times in her heart area.

Baby was blessed.

Only a month ago the land was dry and dusty and every plant was leafless the ground was all brown. There did not seem to be hope. She watched the shamba as the dew on the three-leafed crops shone. The farm now was green with life. Experience had taught her that no matter how severe drought, there would always be good rains after. That tree life will always return and the animals will be jolly again! Was this symbolic of her life?

Mellie felt green and hopeful, despite her old age. She picked up her walking stick and walked to Billy, the - he-goat who was now skinny and toothless. He had been too weak to join the other animals for grazing. She gave him some few cabbage leaves and watched him feed for some moments.

She then took her rosary and started to pray for her offspring. She always wished all her children would be here with her all the time but since she had taught them to work hard for their families, she knew this was not possible. She prayed for them. She was the intercessor of the family as everyone would come and tell her, "Mwaitu, please pray for someone who got burnt. Mwaitu, people in such and such a place are dying of hunger, please pray. Mwaitu, I am sitting for exams and another is looking for a job." The list was endless and so she was always engaged, always praying.

The only one she knew she needn't pray for was Baby. Mellie did, for Mellie prayed for everyone. But she knew Baby would be alright. She knew Baby would be fine.

Reflection Time: The Journey

As you read this what comes to mind?
Is there anything you can be thankful for?

Check within if as you read this book any feeling or pain is being released. Sometimes we are convinced that our happiness lies in our past. Maybe this is partly true. Looking at our past closets just like decluttering helps us heal and allow forth what serves us for the journey. It puts us in control of our choices from now henceforth. We can then appreciate the paths chosen for us with gratitude. Feeling our present and making a conscious decision to live this present life gifted to us implants in us the passion needed to juice life up.

The deepest intention of 'The Change You Want is Within You' is to offer some healing and relief to readers like you and others who can identify with any of the stories herein.

'The Change You Want is Within You' is a blend of many stories sifted through her perceptional filter and in the writer's perspective.

❖

Gratitude.

In the spirit of Africanism my 'I' ness is as a result of our 'We' ness which I am thankful for.

Mothers, for all that you have been to us and to our siblings, thank you.

Thank you for being our mothers. Sorry for the times we take you for granted. We are sorry for the many times we behaved badly and added to your stresses. Sorry on behalf of all children in the world.

We forgive you for the times you did your best which we saw and felt was not good enough. Now we know you did everything in your capacity to equip us with skills to live our lives and that was good work. Thanks.

And now thanks to all the giants living and dead on whose shoulders we stand. Thanks for all the years we spent or continue to spend with our dear mothers and fathers.

Thanks, fathers. May those fathers who have gone ahead of us rest in peace? For those that have hurt us in any way for being absent or otherwise we forgive you. Thanks for giving us life. Thanks for granting us the experiences that have shaped and charted our journey as it is. Thanks for all the special men and women who have made us who we are today.

Thanks for and to all our siblings who have contributed to our being the best of ourselves.

As the sky is blue and the proverbs remain true, remind us to always say thanks for all the great as well as the simple things we enjoy that we sometimes forget to appreciate in our lives!

However, I want to bring you onboard because you matter and need to be proactive in reading this book.

What I do and my expectations;

I am in a facilitative profession and I realize that many times I expect others to come to me and open up and tell me their deepest secrets without being mindful of how difficult it is for them. I know from being in therapy - which I have been privileged to access - that it can be very scary to 'look and be seen' as needing help. I guess others have felt like they were 'undressing' in therapy. It actually at times feels like the following poet puts it.

With half a laugh of hearty zest
I strip me off my coat and vest

Then heeding not, the frigid air
I fling away my underwear

So, having nothing else to doff
I rip my epidermis off.
More secrets to acquaint you with
I pare my bones to strips of pith

And when the expose' is done
I hang, a cobweb skeleton,

While you sit there, aloof, remote
And will not shed your overcoat,

Tom Prideau

However, I realize that other than sit in misery I can choose to get someone with whom I can feel safe (I have worked on my safety for many years and still do) to talk to and work out my issues with. My experience has taught me that working on self requires devotion and total commitment. There is no shortcut to healing but through its process which is not for the fainthearted. Working during sessions as well as outside of counselling times.

This book gives suggestions to you the reader as to what you could do to work through what you are going through. This is what has been helpful to me and while it is not ideal, it offers you another option.

Like the chick in an egg, the time is rife for each of us to do the inside work in order to hatch out. It is hard work as we peck a little at a time from the inside.

And the world is waiting for our hatching!

-THE END-

www.ingramcontent.com/pod-product-compliance
Lightning Source LLC
LaVergne TN
LVHW050541160826
845677LV00011B/2122
9789914700466